TIME
LIFE
BOOKS
®

The Art of Sewing
The Old West
The Emergence of Man
The American Wilderness
The Time-Life Encyclopedia of Gardening
Life Library of Photography
This Fabulous Century
Foods of the World
Time-Life Library of America
Time-Life Library of Art
Great Ages of Man
Life Science Library
The Life History of the United States
Time Reading Program
Life Nature Library
Life World Library
Family Library:
   The Time-Life Book of the Family Car
   The Time-Life Family Legal Guide
   The Time-Life Book of Family Finance

PHOTOGRAPHY YEAR
1974 EDITION
BY THE EDITORS OF TIME-LIFE BOOKS

TIME-LIFE BOOKS, NEW YORK

ON THE COVER: Fresh and lovely expressions of two traditional themes—the landscape and the female form—are juxtaposed here to indicate the artistic accomplishments of photographers in 1973. Joseph Jachna, a newly discovered talent, created the jumbled world of stones and fingers by holding a shaving mirror in front of his lens. The misty portrait of a nubile young girl is from the English photographer David Hamilton's new book *Sisters,* published in 1973.

Contents

EDITORIAL STAFF FOR PHOTOGRAPHY YEAR:

EDITOR: Sheldon Cotler
Text Editors: George Constable, Anne Horan
Staff Writers: Michael Drons, Lee Greene,
John von Hartz, Don Nelson, Michèle Wood
Chief Researcher: Elizabeth D. Meyer
Researchers: Joan Chambers, Jane Coughran,
Lee Hassig, Ruth Kelton, Denise Lynch,
Mary Carroll Marden, Nancy Shuker,
John Conrad Weiser
Assistant Designers: James Eisenman, Marion Flynn

Editorial Production
Production Editor: Douglas B. Graham
Assistant: Gennaro C. Esposito
Quality Director: Robert L. Young
Assistant: James J. Cox
Copy Staff: Rosalind Stubenberg (chief),
Charles Blackwell, Ricki Tarlow, Florence Keith
Picture Department: Dolores A. Littles,
Martin Baldessari

Valuable assistance was given by the following departments and individuals of Time Inc.: Editorial Production, Norman Airey; Library, Benjamin Lightman; Picture Collection, Doris O'Neil; TIME-LIFE Photo Lab, George Karas, Herbert Orth, Albert Schneider; TIME-LIFE News Service, Murray J. Gart; Correspondents Elisabeth Kraemer (Bonn), Frank Iwama (Tokyo), Maria Vincenza Aloisi, Josephine du Brusle and Michèle Berge (Paris), Margot Hapgood and Dorothy Bacon (London), Ann Natanson (Rome), Eva Stichova (Prague), Mary Johnson (Stockholm), Eidur Gudnason (Reykjavik), Roy Rutter (Madrid), Friso Endt (Amsterdam), John Dunn (Melbourne), Bing W. Wong (Hong Kong), Felix Rosenthal (Moscow), Peter Rehak (Ottawa), Martha Green (San Francisco), Richard Woodbury (Chicago).

It sometimes seems that progress in photography is lethargic and the year-to-year changes microscopic. The first book related to photography was written in 1558 by Giovanni Battista Della Porta, who called his work *Natural Magic;* it dealt with the predecessor of the camera, the room-sized sketching aid called a camera obscura. It has taken four centuries for Della Porta's magic process to metamorphose from a dark booth with a small hole in one wall into the intricate, portable picture-taking camera of today. The evolution of photographic art has not been quite so protracted, but it did require more than a hundred years to establish itself as the preeminent visual commentator of the 20th Century.

Change there is, nonetheless—often significant change that can be recognized only by critical examination at regular intervals. This volume strives to provide such a review.

In technology, some developments that seemed at first to be almost routine improvements could have long-range impact: a big step forward in the design of multielement lenses may be in the making, thanks to better coating techniques, and, separately, new color printing methods could alter the entire approach to color by shifting emphasis from the lab-processed transparency to the individually produced print.

Artistic events also offered surprises. An exhibition at a small-town museum in Germany was ostensibly devoted to the photographic antecedents of one avant-garde school of painting, but actually related photography to all modern painting and provided perhaps the best and clearest explanation yet seen of the interaction between the two arts.

Another show, in one of the world's most prestigious institutions, New York City's Museum of Modern Art, found in the everyday news picture succinct expression of basics of communication.

Everywhere—in books, in portfolios from new photographers, in the "takes" brought back from assignments—photographs themselves showed trends in portraiture, documentation, landscape. Even the marketplace was in ferment; a survey of the professional world suggests how it may be affected by the flood of newly trained photographers now graduating from university courses. These newcomers, together with the ideas, events and pictures recorded on the following pages, generated dramatic progress in the face and the technology of photography, making 1973 a meaningful year for all of those who are involved in the art.

The Editors

The Documentary

Documentary photographs record people and the world they live in, but in a way that says something fresh and pertinent. The selections from 1973 could serve to define this field. Two qualities of the human character are examined. Neal Slavin explores, in a series of wry group pictures, the way clubs and organizations meet each human's need for a special relationship with some of his fellow beings. A male photographer, Garry Winogrand, makes a candid appraisal of women at the very time they are reassessing their opinion of themselves and their role in society. The documentary view of nature reveals a nightmare as Pete Turner shows a tiny island helpless in the grip of a volcanic upheaval.

Aligned in a single gesture of rapt patriotism, ▶ uniformed members of a Long Island Veterans of Foreign Wars post salute the American flag. The open Bible, and the post's trophies for marching and sports activities arrayed on the table, further define the common values of the group.

The Sgt. Harvey L. Miller Post, VFW, Baldwin, New York

A Sense of Belonging

To explain the remarkable photographic odyssey that he began in 1973, Neal Slavin quotes an observation by the 19th Century French Traveler Alexis de Tocqueville: "The Americans of all ages, all conditions and all dispositions constantly form associations." Slavin's fascination with this national trait was triggered by a casual glance at a picture of his brother-in-law in a Boy Scout troop. The image of the uniformed youngsters, full of jaunty companionship, set him thinking about the many ways in which people gather in groups to pursue shared interests. Here, he realized, was an unsung mode of identity, begging for photographic exploration. Since then, he has hired a professional researcher to help him locate clubs, societies and associations of all kinds, ranging from the familiar Veterans of Foreign Wars *(preceding page)* to such exotica as a group whose special interest is the art of making grotesque faces *(page 19)*. He has already made photographs of about 50 organizations, and he plans hundreds more. Ultimately, they will be compiled in book form.

Slavin sometimes speaks of his pictures as record photographs—an assessment that is true enough, but incomplete. He takes strobe-lighting equipment with him on his visits to group meetings, and sets up his gear to create the ambience familiar in routine commercial pictures. He shoots with negative color film and, like an increasing number of artist-photographers, makes his own color prints so that he can closely control the results (see pages 190-195 for more on color printing). The finished prints bear only a superficial resemblance to the bland grouped faces that hang on clubhouse walls. These documents go beyond the recording of a related selection of human beings; they show the emotional rewards of that relationship. "Every group has its own identity," says Slavin. "Being special is the whole point, and that sense of specialness is what I am trying to show in these pictures —the meaning of belonging as well as the fact of belonging."

To release this emotional dimension, Slavin puts each group in its natural habitat. He asks his subjects to wear their uniforms, caps, ribbons or pins; he surrounds them with the official trappings of the organization—flags, banners, charters, plaques and awards. In some instances he shows them performing their chosen work. The resulting pictures brim with human feelings. Blind senior citizens hold up their handicrafts with an air of quiet pride *(page 16);* sets of twins *(page 14)* delight in the distinction of being two of a kind. Individuals are not submerged in a group; instead, the group strengthens them by giving them a larger self. Slavin is continually astonished by the variety of the group-selves that are delineated in his documents. "When I first started out," he says, "I wasn't sure how long the project would sustain itself, but now I'm more excited than ever. The more group pictures I take, the less repetitive they seem."

This society, originally founded to study California's forests, evolved into one devoted to the economic and social welfare of its members, providing them with such benefits as group life insurance. Slavin's portrait of a meeting held in a New York union hall is centered on a picture of a benefactress who bequeathed her house as a retirement home for incapacitated members.

The Lady Dorothy Circle, Companions of the Forest of America, Jamaica, New York

International Twins Convention, Springfield, Illinois

This lighthearted view of a convention of twins reflects the admission of one of the participants that "Twins are natural hams." Nearly every one of the hundreds of twins at the convention volunteered to pose for the picture, but Slavin drew the line at 23 pairs—all enjoying the chance to show off how special they are.

To convey the shared interest of a horticultural ▶ organization specializing in begonias and other shade-loving plants, photographer Slavin posed the members under the cheesecloth screen covering a garden at the Los Angeles Arboretum. He then shot the picture through the glass of a greenhouse, creating dim, ghostly reflections.

Senior Citizens, Associated Blind, Inc., New York City

◀ *A group of elderly blind people, joined by a resolve to be self-sufficient and productive in spite of their disability, show the results of their handiwork: dolls, colored-glass flowers, mosaic bowls and weaving. The uplifted face of the man seated at right shines with pride in their accomplishments together, as the fingers of one hand read the raised dots on a page of Braille.*

Practicing for the real thing, volunteer firemen prepare to dash into the smoke-filled entrance of their training building. Slavin chose a training session for the picture because it suggested the danger that welds the men together—and yet the danger was not so real as to overshadow the obvious camaraderie of the group.

Empire Hose Company No. 3, Baldwin, New York

Cemetery Workers, New York City

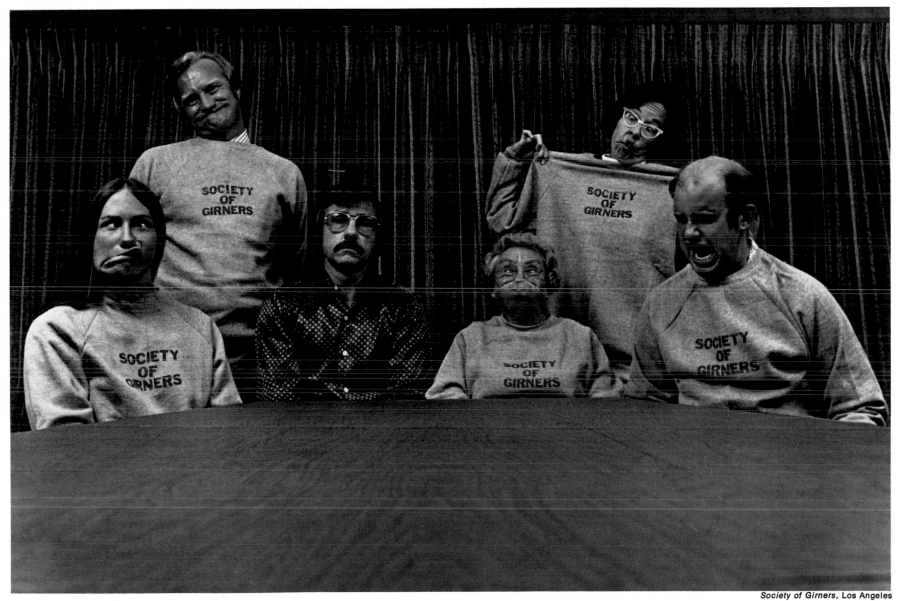

Society of Girners, Los Angeles

◄ Pausing during their work after a funeral, gravediggers reveal a quality that unites them as like individuals and sets them apart as a group —matter-of-fact ease in the presence of death.

Named for the Scottish word that means "to snarl," the Society of Girners practices its arcane art of face-making, led by a 72-year-old grandmother who can swallow her nose. The group came into being as a result of a contest held by TV performer Gary Owens, who sits here straight-faced among the muggers.

Inferno on an Island

On January 23, 1973, a resident on the small Icelandic island of Heimaey was driving into the town of Vestmannaeyjar when he noticed flames flickering on the skyline. He alerted the fire department, but the firemen quickly realized that this blaze could not be extinguished by human hands. It was, in fact, the first hot breath of a volcano that soon split open the earth, built an enormous cone and began to rain destruction on the town.

When photographer Pete Turner read about the town's peril in a New York newspaper, he quickly wangled an assignment to document the event and flew to the scene aboard a special press flight—only to be told that all press representatives would have to leave because of the hazardous conditions. Turner, however, was accompanied by an Icelandic author; his companion interceded with the mayor and won him permission to stay. For 26 hours he was the only photographer on the island, witnessing the eruption at the height of its fury. The inhabitants of the town had already been evacuated, and Turner spent his first night bedded down in an abandoned house. He could not sleep, for lava bombs—golf-ball-sized rocks with red-hot cores—beat a steady tattoo on the roof and the plywood boards nailed over the windows. "It was like trying to sleep inside a kettle drum," he recalled. At dawn, he went into the backyard to photograph the volcano's awesome fireworks *(opposite);* then he wandered through the doomed town.

He felt as though he had entered a realm of science fiction. Close by the town, the newly formed cone continued to belch fire, gases and lava bombs. Buildings and roads were buried under cinders. Smoke and steam billowed across the sky. At times the ground "shook like jello," and he had to wear a steel helmet as protection against the rock missiles falling from the sky. Even the light had a tenuous, end-of-the-world quality. At that latitude and season, daylight lasted only six hours, and the sun lay so close to the horizon that dawn seemed to blend directly into dusk.

In this dull, ominous light, Turner created a series of pictures that could be a vision of the apocalypse. People are entirely absent from his photographs. The desolate landscape, seared and tortured, seems to verge on the abstract—an effect the photographer achieved by slightly underexposing most of his shots. The underexposure transformed the drifts of dark ash and pumice into black shapes, lacking in detail and depth. It also caused the hues to become more saturated, resulting in bold blocks and strokes of color that further add to the impression of a surreal world, transmuted in a terrible smithy. For some pictures, Turner altered the normal color balance with filter and film: in the image opposite, for example, he placed heavy emphasis on cool blue tones to dramatize the monstrous violation of this arctic land by volcanic fire. As interpreted by Turner's camera, nature is frighteningly unnatural. Landscape has become deathscape.

Pristine even in its hour of agony, the Icelandic town of Vestmannaeyjar is engulfed by volcanic debris. Pete Turner climbed a nearby mountain and fitted his 35mm SLR with a long focal-length 400mm lens to get this overview. By the end of 1973 the volcano was quiet, and about a quarter of the town's 5,000 inhabitants had returned.

The new volcano looming over the town heralds dawn with a blast of fire and molten rock. Turner took advantage of the momentary absence of clouds to deepen the blue of the sky by shooting the picture with a blue filter and indoor film. The film, which is designed to balance the red shades predominant in incandescent light, responds strongly to blue and thus gives a blue cast to pictures that are shot outdoors.

Underexposing to obliterate detail in the dark drifts of volcanic debris, Turner generated a sense of encroaching oblivion in images of an abandoned fisherman's house (above) and an isolated, forlorn park bench (opposite).

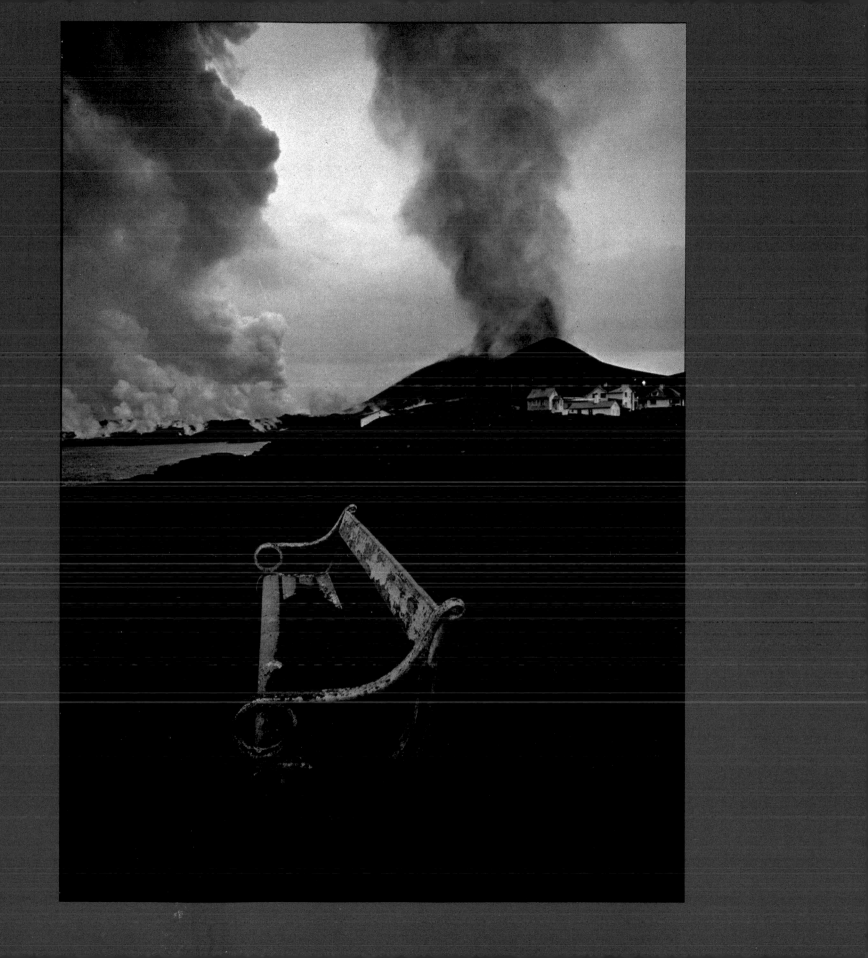

Rooftops, eaves and corners of houses protrude
from nightmare-black drifts of ash and pumice.
Underexposure transformed the debris into pure
shape and contour, and the lack of shadows, due
to heavy clouds overhead, helped to create
an abstract two-dimensional appearance.

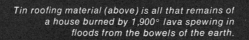

Tin roofing material (above) is all that remains of a house burned by 1,900° lava spewing in floods from the bowels of the earth.

When lava flows to the shore and meets the sea, it sends up billows of steam (right), which Turner deftly portrayed as a violent, blurred explosion by making a long exposure.

A Candid Look at Women

Photography is not always honest with women. The camera has been used to idealize and romanticize them, seeking moments when traditional conceptions of feminine grace and behavior are most clearly realized—often with stunningly beautiful results *(pages 58-61)*. But in 1973, one photographer, Garry Winogrand, documented his appreciation of the female sex in a series of candid pictures that managed to combine a male view of women as women with a more fundamental view of them as people. Winogrand has gathered these pictures together for a book that he first titled *Women Are Beautiful.* But when his teen-age daughter accused him of a chauvinistic outlook, he added a subtitle: *The Observations of a Male Chauvinist Pig.*

"I have always loved to watch women," Winogrand admits. "I have a compulsion about taking pictures of attractive women." But if a compulsive element is there, so is honesty. Winogrand does not impose any definition of beauty on his subjects, nor does he insist on placing his subjects in a glamorous or flattering setting. He simply reacts whenever a woman catches his eye, composing the picture instinctively and shooting quickly. Women are shown waiting at a bus stop, walking along a sidewalk, chatting in a phone booth, lounging in a restaurant. Some of his subjects are flustered and coy, unabashedly acting out roles that now are considered outmoded stereotypes. Others are shown in natural and unself-conscious postures that once were considered suitable only for men. Still others are caught in mid-blink or mid-scowl or in unaffected, relaxed joy. Spontaneity is the essence of Winogrand's working method, and, while the resulting images are sometimes disconcerting, they are never artificial.

The interaction between men and women is very much alive in these frank, straightforward images. Indeed, it is brought to life by being allowed to operate on its own terms, whenever and however that may be. The women in Garry Winogrand's pictures are not too good to be true; they are real. Because he has not posed them, simply recorded them as they are, their beauty comes naturally.

The Year's Books

Every year, books on photography increase in number and variety, and the 1973 crop was counted in the hundreds. The books ranged in price from 95 cents to 85 dollars, in dimensions from pocket to coffee-table size, in subject matter from the famous (opposite) to the anonymous, and in photographic approach from the glamorous to the bluntly candid. One difference this year was that many outstanding books seemed to consist of collections of the works of several photographers—a shift from last year, when notable volumes concentrated on individual photographers.

In this tightly cropped portrait of Greta Garbo as ▶ the German spy Mata Hari, Clarence Bull caught the cunning and passion that the Swedish star brought to the role. The picture appears on the jacket of "Grand Illusions," a new book celebrating the still photography that fostered the glamour and excitement of Hollywood's heyday.

CLARENCE S. BULL: *Greta Garbo*, 1932

"Grand Illusions"

In the wonderland that once was Hollywood, stars were not born or discovered—they were made. And much of the task of sustaining their position in the firmament of moviedom fell to a group of talented but little-known photographers who produced torrents of still photographs to publicize the stars and their roles. The 233 black-and-white pictures in *Grand Illusions,* though a tiny fraction of these photographers' total production, illustrate the skill of these men at catching and augmenting a star's appeal, or subtly evoking the feeling of an entire movie role—be it mystery, romance, adventure or sophisticated villainy.

Grand Illusions spans the heyday of Hollywood, from the 1920s to the late 1940s. During these years, every major studio retained a staff of still photographers and provided them with extensive working space—called galleries—complete with backdrops, props, costumes and crews of make-up artists, technicians and wardrobe mistresses. The pictures were made with big studio view cameras producing 8 x 10 negatives—large enough so that they could readily be retouched to add or subtract practically any part of the human physiognomy. Noses were straightened, jowls removed and figures improved. No offending hair, wrinkle or blemish escaped the retoucher's pencil and airbrush. In some portraits, not a single square inch of real skin remains.

Stars were obliged by their contracts to spend whole days at the photographers' galleries. When not filming a movie they sat for the glamour portraits that were gobbled up by the ubiquitous fan magazines of the era, or they posed for the large, glossy head shots that were mailed out by the thousands to adoring fans. (In the early '30s, more than 32 million fan letters deluged Hollywood studios every year.) And in the midst of a film, the stars used off time to go to the gallery, along with costumes and props, to be photographed in "costume portraits," which were used to advertise the movie of the moment in newspapers and theater-lobby posters.

For the most part the work was anonymous—*Grand Illusions* does not name any photographers. Some of their output can be identified, however, with the help of Hollywood oldtimers. They remember well such outstanding practitioners as Clarence Bull—Greta Garbo *(page 39)* would let no one else take her picture—and George Hurrell, a freelance who received as much as $1,000 per sitting for glamorizing superstars like Joan Bennett *(page 42).* In any case, it was a short-lived art form. In the 1950s television crippled Hollywood. Fewer stars appeared, a dwindling number of fans wrote for portraits of their favorites and movie magazines chose more realistic, candid images. But the fantasy, thrill and glamour of Hollywood were a charming chapter of America's past, and they are deftly recaptured in these photographs.

GRAND ILLUSIONS
By Richard Lawton with a text by Hugo Leckey.
255 pages. McGraw-Hill Book Company, New York, 1973. $20.

Mirrored in a prop on the set of "The Lily and the Rose," Lillian Gish portrays the rejected lily in this early melodrama. The star, still active in the theater today, made four other films in 1915, including "The Birth of a Nation."

PHOTOGRAPHER UNKNOWN: *Lillian Gish*, 1915

GEORGE HURRELL: *Joan Bennett, 1935*

With highlights and shadows playing on her flawless hair and dress, Joan Bennett poses in a moment of serenity for a 1935 "glamour portrait." Asked about the picture 38 years later, she recalled: "It was my own dress and I loved it."

A portrait of the stars of ''Morocco'' exudes a sense of faraway adventure and blighted romance with only a plain backdrop, costumes, a chair —and the talented impersonations of an insolent Cooper and a sultry Dietrich.

EUGENE ROBERT RICHEE: *Gary Cooper and Marlene Dietrich*, 1930

43

Framed in a shaft of light and impeccably groomed, even a heavy like James Cagney, the gangster of "The Public Enemy," becomes a respectable star in this publicity portrait.

Katharine Hepburn effortlessly projects feminine ▶ charm through her disguise as a young man for a role in "Sylvia Scarlet." But despite the photographer's best efforts and the talent of the star, the movie was a colossal failure.

PHOTOGRAPHER UNKNOWN: *James Cagney*, 1933

44

ERNEST A. BACHRACH: *Katharine Hepburn*, 1935

45

"The Black Photographers Annual 1973"

The inaugural edition of *The Black Photographers Annual 1973* is a remarkable demonstration of unity operating amidst diversity. The black photographers who conceived and executed the book set out only to find and publish exceptional photographs. Forty-nine different black photographers contributed 120 black-and-white prints to the issue. In addition to acknowledged masters such as the widely honored freelance photographer Roy DeCarava, and the grand octogenarian James Van DerZee, who is represented by a group of photographs taken during the early decades of this century, there are less well known but noteworthy portraitists of black youth, such as Rennie George *(right)* and interpreters of jazz musicians such as Clarence E. Eastmond *(opposite).* The styles include realistic photojournalism, composite photographs, manipulated prints, time exposures, carefully posed portraits and images that freeze peaks of action. And the subject matter ranges widely across the world of black America, from spirited concerts to violent civil-rights demonstrations to sedate reflections in an oily street.

Yet, despite the variety of the collection, the images in *The Black Photographers Annual* have one vital element in common. Nearly all of them manifest a high degree of empathy on the part of the photographers. The men and women who took these pictures are intimately knowledgeable about the joys and pains of black people, the dynamics of black society and the sensory nuances of life in city streets or on a sharecropper's farm. They are insiders, participants—and, as such, they do not judge their world or force it into any particular mold. Instead, they simply observe it in a spirit of honest affirmation—much the same way another distinguished book published in 1973 depicts the suburban world of white middle America *(pages 50-53).* For example, there is nothing exaggerated about the self-assurance of the teen-age lad at right, for neither he nor the photographer had to prove anything: they understood and respected one another. The same quality of dignity and natural worth is caught whenever and wherever these photographers look at their people. Even dilapidated tenements, subway stations, concrete playgrounds or alleyways are viewed with fond familiarity. Thus, *The Black Photographers Annual* is more than an exploration of a world—it is a homecoming as well.

RENNIE GEORGE

In a portrait rendered almost sculptural by sidelighting, a black teenager stares back at the photographer's camera with an air of quiet confidence that seems utterly natural.

THE BLACK PHOTOGRAPHERS ANNUAL 1973
Foreword by Toni Morrison. Introduction by
Clayton Riley. Joe Crawford, Editor. 144 pages.
Black Photographers Annual, Inc., Brooklyn, New
York, 1972. Hardbound, $10.95. Softbound, $5.95.

Saxophonist Sonny Rollins appears to vibrate across the stage of Manhattan's Town Hall in a time exposure that captures the kinetic energies and emotions of a jazz concert.

THERON TAYLOR

The blur of motion and sun rays play against wood patterns in this bewildering image. A figure bounds up a staircase and out of sight, leaving a mystery in the shadowed hallway: Why the haste?

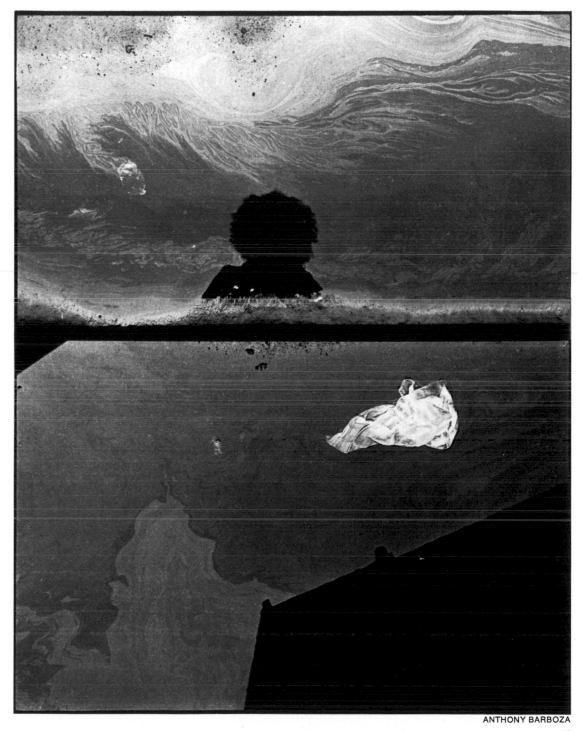

In a composite of two pictures, the photographer and a building are reflected in an oily New York street, and someone's dropped handkerchief has become a cloud in a murky sky.

ANTHONY BARBOZA

49

Bill Owens: "Suburbia"

SUBURBIA
By Bill Owens. 108 pages. Straight Arrow Books,
San Francisco, 1973. Distributed by Quick Fox
Inc., New York. Hardbound, $15.00. Softbound, $6.95.

"This book is about my friends and the world I live in," says photographer Bill Owens in the opening statement of his book *Suburbia.* Indeed, his pictures embody the best qualities of friendship and citizenship. He neither flatters suburbia nor does he denigrate it. Instead, he presents the life style with scrupulous clarity and allows it to stand on its own merits. The people, in fact, testify in their own behalf, for he has used their comments for the book's captions.

Suburbia is California's Livermore Amador Valley—40 minutes by freeway southeast of San Francisco. In the past decade the valley's vineyards have given way to thousands of comfortable homes for young, basically secure families. As Owens says, "They have realized the American Dream. They are proud to be home owners and to have achieved material success."

Owens himself is a relative newcomer to the suburban world. He grew up on a farm, graduated from a small state college, hitchhiked around the world and spent two years with the Peace Corps in the West Indies before he took a job in 1968 as a staff photographer for the Livermore *Independent,* a local newspaper. His first confrontation with the casual prosperity of the valley was a jarring one—"I suffered from culture shock," he recalls. But shock changed to fascination as his job brought him into the homes and lives of suburbia, and in 1971 he began to assemble a photographic record of his impressions. He brought his camera to parties, and he even placed advertisements in his newspaper—"Please call me if I can photograph you, your family, your home. . . ." Two years later, he spread out several hundred prints on a gymnasium floor and made the choice of 126 that were to become *Suburbia* (a smaller selection was entered in the LIFE bicentennial contest, portions of which appear on pages 169-177, and Owens won third prize for professionals).

Owens' presentation of suburbia is all-encompassing and lavishly informative. He moves from living rooms to kitchens to bathrooms to bedrooms; he stares into cupboards, drawers, refrigerators; he investigates garages and backyards. Beyond their cozy homes Owens shows his fellow suburbanites enjoying such community get-togethers as neighborhood Christmas caroling and a Fourth of July block party *(opposite).* All of the pictures were taken with an SLR that produces a negative 2¼ inches x 2¾ inches, large enough to capture detail a 35mm camera might miss. The sharpness of Owens' pictures allows the viewer to see every blade of grass in the pampered lawns, every nuance of gesture or expression, and even the titles of magazines on a living-room table. Inevitably, the camera catches the darker aspects of the suburban subculture, too—the conformity and conspicuous consumption. Yet the net effect is distinctly positive. The people in these pictures enjoy suburbia; they are glad to be there, and Owens is too.

"People throw away a lot of good things: clothes, toys, broken toasters, record players and in the newer areas they throw out tables and chairs that don't fit in their new house. The ecology movement doesn't matter. I make over $250 in coke bottles. People here can't realize there are poor people in the world. They can't think about the needs of other people."

"This is our second annual Fourth of July block party. This year thirty-three families came for beer, barbequed chicken, corn on the cob, potato salad, green salad, macaroni salad and watermelon. After eating and drinking we staged our parade and fireworks."

"We really enjoy getting together with
our friends to drink and dance. It's a wild party
and we're having a great time."

"I wanted Christina to learn some responsibility
for cleaning her room, but it didn't work."

"I enjoy giving a Tupperware party in my home. It gives me a chance to talk to my friends. But really, Tupperware is a homemaker's dream, you save time and money because your food keeps longer."

"Our house is built with the living room in the back, so in the evenings we sit out front of the garage and watch the traffic go by."

"The Family Album"

Around the turn of the century, two young men in the town of Buckfield, Maine, bought a camera—an inexpensive box that used cumbersome 4 x 5-inch glass plates—and began to take snapshots of their families and friends. To Gilbert Tilton and Fred Record, photography was a diversion—a delightful and easy means of catching life on the wing. After taking about 150 pictures, they put aside their camera and took up more serious pursuits, first running a carriage shop, then a bicycle shop, then the town's first garage. They died in the 1960s, and except for 10 faded prints in a dusty album, the snapshots of their youth were forgotten. This book, *The Family Album,* retrieves those images and re-creates the uncomplicated joy of being young in a small New England community several generations ago.

The book was assembled by a Maine photographer, Mark Silber, who saw the 10 faded prints in a Buckfield grocery store run by the son of Gilbert Tilton. Silber was immediately taken with the pictures' casual but acute perception of that long-ago world, and he asked if the negatives still existed. They did—and, in fact, the younger Tilton dug up several dozen others in his barn. Later, Fred Record's nephew found still more negatives neatly stored in their original boxes, some of which bore the eerie expiration warning: "Develop before 1901."

Silber made contact prints from 45 of the negatives, then identified the scenes by showing them to the son and nephew of the photographers. The two men, who themselves have been friends for nearly half a century, began to reminisce about the people and places caught in the snapshots. Their dialogue, recorded by Silber and used as captions in the book, as they are in the pages following, draws the past close again, breathing life and meaning back into these two-dimensional mementos of a long-departed era. A millpond that disappeared years earlier in a flood reappears along with memories of many hours spent fishing there—memories that happen to belong to the descendants of the photographers, yet could easily be the reminiscences of the photographers themselves. Old bicycles, barns, derby hats and Sunday topcoats with fur collars are lovingly recalled. Occasionally, the musings turn regretful when something in the pictures cannot be identified; but, for the most part, the dialogue with the past is uncannily intimate, as though 70 years ago was yesterday.

The Family Album is more than nostalgia; it is superb social documentary, made possible by the development of simple photographic equipment late in the 19th Century. Thereafter thousands of ordinary people like Gilbert Tilton and Fred Record began leaving realistic, relaxed and highly personal records of their lives for the generations to come. Mark Silber discovered a few lovely but limited pictures, but his book shows just how greatly photography democratized—and enriched—our sense of the past.

THE FAMILY ALBUM
Photographs of the 1890s and 1900s by Gilbert Wight Tilton and Fred W. Record. Assembled by Mark Silber. 95 pages. David R. Godine, Boston, 1973. $15.00.

◄ "That's my dad.

Like a thunderbird in a snow.

**That's right. They jump up in the air and spread-
eagle their arms and legs and someone snapped
a picture of him no doubt.**

*Backdrop. . . . It must have been wintertime. I
can't imagine how he got that white effect, can you?*

**Time exposure? What do you think—it's snow on
the ground with a white sky?**

*He's laying on the snowbank, I think. And I guess
they did it upside down to make him right side up."*

*"Now that one we know about. That house is gone.
The river is still there.
There—you name those off, Tilton.*

**Left to right, George Brown, Babe Wood, and Will
Record. They're sawing the ice on Nezinscot River
just about where the former railroad bridge was.**

*That was a mill pond there. You could saw ice
there where now it's just a rapids. There was a
dam right under the railroad bridge. That went out
with the high waters. Probably in 1936, wasn't it?*

**I fished up there many hours at a time before it
went. It was an unusual dam. The other dams
were on the river below the village and they were
of granite. This one was made of logs that were
crisscrossed and notched and staked.**

Yeah, that's gone. That's departed."

"That's Rebecca L. Probably just before she went upstairs to go to bed. Her hair all down.

Very sexy. She's probably 15 or 16 there.

They were living down in the John Damon place.

What do you call the John Damon place?

Well, John Damon used to live there. Old John."

"Oh yes, here we go. That's Dot. Dressed up in the clothes of their men, I guess.

You think that's Sadie Maxim? That's Dot.

This is Sadie. I'd say dressed up in their husbands' clothes.

They probably were married by that time. That's at the pond all right. Hm, they are pretty good lookers. Really—weren't they? Hair right underneath their hats.

They probably spent some time . . .

Oh yeah, they probably put in hours at that.

Didn't spare any details.

Nope, everything was there, pipe and all. Women might do that today, possibly. Gee, not too many years ago some guy dressed up in those women's things, posed as a patient in a doctor's office and just barely got by. . . ."

"Dot and Sadie having a little joyous spring dance there. I'd like to know where that place is. One thing I can tell you for sure. That's a Franklin stove. It says so right on the bottom."

"That's a birthday party at Dr. Arthur Cole's home.
Who's the one with the dust cap?
That's either Helen or Margaret Shaw.
Oh yeah. I knew I've seen her. It was either Helen's birthday, or Arthur's birthday, or Sadie's birthday.
Well, that was before my time."

David Hamilton: "Sisters"

Among the best-selling books of 1973 was *Sisters,* by the English photographer David Hamilton. It consists entirely of photographs of young women, and it was certain to raise the hackles of militant feminists—or of anyone who rejects outmoded notions about the female role. For these girls are viewed unabashedly as sex objects. Hamilton's photographs belong to the tradition of pinups and magazine fold-outs, and from less skillful hands they could easily have turned out to be nothing more than commercial hackwork. Hamilton made them pictures of astonishing beauty, evincing a feeling for the expressive power of light and a flair for romantic staging that mark him as a photographer of extraordinary talent.

Hamilton himself gives much of the credit for the quality of the results to his models. He says he spends much more time looking for subjects than in making photographs. He haunts beaches, college campuses and cafés, mostly in Scandinavia, seeking out healthy-looking adolescents. They must, he explains, exhibit a blend of "timidity, candor and grace." Preferably they should have fine blond hair—when backlighted it creates a romantically golden halo. Hamilton's own sensitivity and a carefully worked out photographic technique do the rest.

The soft, warm atmosphere of Hamilton's pictures is compounded of several elements. He shoots in early morning light to mute the colors. He uses high-speed color film, which is slightly grainy. Both the gentle light and the film characteristics diffuse the image to achieve a misty effect, but Hamilton decries the use of screens or special lens attachments.

The settings, too, reinforce the quietly sensual mood. Hamilton studied architecture and interior design before becoming a photographer, and his acquaintance with these two disciplines shows up in the atmospheric staging of the pictures. Many were taken at one or the other of the two country houses that he maintains in Denmark and on the French Riviera. His props are old-fashioned—the wicker chairs, gauzy curtains, flowered wallpaper and gilt-framed mirrors that suggest an idealized past of a lyrical daydream. The result is pure fantasy, but fantasy such as few photographs conjure.

SISTERS
By David Hamilton. Text by Alain Robbe-Grillet.
142 pages. William Morrow & Company, Inc.,
1973. $15.95.

A young woman gazes dreamily into the distance, absorbed in secret reveries, in one of David Hamilton's studies of feminine beauty.

Two girls pause together on a rural roadside, seemingly shy and pensive after sharing some personal thoughts.

*Three look-alike young girls make a
casual, uncohesive crowd—clustered together,
yet separated by their private musings.*

As two girls nap on an old-fashioned coverlet, their softly focused forms harmonize with the embroidery and fleecy fabric of the bed clothes.

"Looking at Photographs"

This book will not tell Everything You Always Wanted to Know about Photography, but it is a good start. Its 100 photographs—most of them unfamiliar and all of them great—make up a fast-paced survey of the art from its beginnings to the present day. The pictures are arranged more or less chronologically to show shifts in style and technique over the 130-odd years of photography's existence, and each is accompanied by a small essay discussing the image itself, the photographer who made it and the time in which it was made.

In this broad sampling of photographers' work, such obscure names as E. J. Bellocq *(page 64)* appear with the more celebrated ones, like Peter Henry Emerson *(opposite),* for the book is not just a showcase for the famous and the prolific; it is rather an attempt to explore the medium and show how it evolved, sometimes in steps taken by little-known practitioners who by lucky accident or instinctive good taste and imagination make worthwhile advances. Not all of the pictures were intended as art by the photographers who made them. Some were meant to teach, reform or sell merchandise. What the pictures share is high quality; each marks a genuine contribution to the medium of photography.

Both the diversity of subject matter and the level of quality in these pictures are largely owed to their source: the comprehensive collection of New York's Museum of Modern Art. Indicating the richness of this great archive was a principal aim of the book, which was prepared by the director of the museum's Department of Photography, John Szarkowski. The museum began acquiring photographs 44 years ago—the first major art repository in the United States to accord this recognition to photographers—and it was also the first to mount a large-scale photographic exhibition, "Photographs of 19th Century Houses" by Walker Evans in 1933. Today it owns more than 10,000 prints; many of them have never been published, and, except at times of special exhibits, they are not on view on the museum's walls. The book's justification is in its title, *Looking at Photographs,* for the pictures in the collection seldom get looked at by the public. And they are, indeed, well worth looking at.

LOOKING AT PHOTOGRAPHS
100 Pictures from the Collection of The Museum of Modern Art. By John Szarkowski. 216 pages. The Museum of Modern Art, New York, 1973. (Distributed by New York Graphic Society, Greenwich, Connecticut.) Hardbound, $15; Softbound, $9.50.

PETER HENRY EMERSON: *Poling the Marsh Hay,* 1886

In a pastoral scene evoking the earthy scent of north-country England and the character of the folk who lived off its land, this pioneer photographer combined ethnographic study with artistic sensibility—and created a picture not unlike those done by painters of his day.

E. J. BELLOCQ: *New Orleans Prostitute*, 1912

A prostitute lazes in calm repose, her unadorned leotard contrasting with the plush setting of her working quarters. Similar pictures of the girls of the French Quarter red-light district were a secret hobby of Bellocq, a commercial photographer considered eccentric but respectable—the strange portraits were found after he died.

In darkness pierced by an ambiguous shaft of ▶ light, a girl considers her face in a hand mirror and quietly combs her hair. Behind her the fringe of a shawl grazes the floor like a crab's pincers—a suggestion of lurking menace in an otherwise tranquil scene, and the touch that marks it as an Alvarez Bravo photograph.

MANUEL ALVAREZ BRAVO: *Woman Combing Her Hair*, 1937

BARBARA MORGAN: *Spring on Madison Square,* 1938

A striding dancer and shadows of fresh spring
tulips contrast with weary pedestrians slogging
through snow in this montage. The photographer
shot the street scene from her window, double-
exposing to get the ghostly images of the walkers
(lower left), then she combined its negative
with that of the dancer and printed both on paper
across which she had laid the flowers.

WILLIAM KLEIN: *Moscow*, 1959

*In three separate planes tied together by
the photographer's vision, contrasts have the
casual spontaneity of a snapshot. On a Moscow
beach a girl steps into the foreground in
mid-laugh, while behind her an old man snoozes
in private melancholy, and still farther in
the background a matronly figure, blissfully
unconcerned, tugs at her stocking.*

Other Books

Of the photography books published in 1973, the editors especially recommend the following.

Current Work

FEW COMFORTS OR SURPRISES:
THE ARKANSAS DELTA
By Eugene Richards, MIT Press, Cambridge, Mass. 123 pages. $9.95. A report on the poverty of southeastern Arkansas.

IMAGE TIBET
By Charles Berger. Artisan Press, Mill Valley, Calif. (Distributed by the Scrimshaw Press, San Francisco.) 76 pages. $25.00. An outstanding work of reproduction containing 30 silkscreen prints in color, made from photographs of the Tibetan Buddhist refugee settlements in northern India.

LANDSCAPES
By Burk Uzzle. Magnum Publications, New York. (Distributed by Light Impressions, Rochester, N.Y.) 96 pages. Hardbound, $14.95; softbound, $6.95. Black-and-white photographs of visual patterns of the American scene.

MINAMATA: LIFE—SACRED AND PROFANE
By W. Eugene Smith with Aileen Smith. Soju-sha, Tokyo publisher. (Distributed by Witkin Gallery, New York.) $7.50. A portfolio of 12 photographs of victims of mercury poisoning in the Japanese city of Minamata.

RAPA NUI
By Fred Picker with a historical summary by Thor Heyerdahl. Two Continents Publishing Corp., New York. 142 pages. $14.95. Photographs and history of Easter Island.

SHOOTING STARS
Edited by Annie Leibovitz. Straight Arrow Books, San Francisco. 159 pages. $9.95. A collection of photographs of rock musicians.

CHARLES A. SWEDLUND PHOTOGRAPHS
Anna Press, Cobden, Ill. Unnumbered pages. $6.50. Multiple exposures with the figure.

THE WEST
By David R. Phillips. Henry Regnery Company, Chicago. 232 pages. $25.00. The settling of the western United States from 1859 to 1900 seen through careful prints made from the author's collection of glass wet-plate negatives.

WISCONSIN DEATH TRIP
By Michael Lesy. Random House, New York. Unnumbered pages. Hardbound, $15,00; softbound, $5.95. A collection of photographs, newspaper clippings and writings centering on a small Wisconsin town from 1885 to 1900.

Retrospectives

ALFRED STIEGLITZ, AN AMERICAN SEER
By Dorothy Norman. Random House, New York. 254 pages. $35.00. A biography with 80 Stieglitz photographs and numerous illustrations of his life.

THE BEST OF LIFE
TIME-LIFE BOOKS, New York. 304 pages. $19.95. A collection of some 700 photographs from the pages of LIFE.

WYNN BULLOCK
Edited by Liliane De Cock, text by Barbara Bullock-Wilson. Morgan and Morgan Inc., Dobbs Ferry, N.Y. 160 pages. $12.00. A representative selection of Bullock's work, including some little-known prints.

CAMERA WORK: A CRITICAL ANTHOLOGY
Edited by Jonathan Green. Aperture Inc., Millerton, N.Y. 376 pages. $25.00. Selections from Alfred Stieglitz' photographic quarterly illustrating the evolution of the avant-garde in American art and photography from 1903 to 1917.

IN THIS PROUD LAND
By Roy Emerson Stryker and Nancy Wood. New York Graphic Society, Greenwich, Conn. 192 pages. $15.00. A collection of the famous Farm Security Administration photographs of rural America, made between 1935 and 1943, that set a style for the documentary.

MEN WITHOUT MASKS
By August Sander, New York Graphic Society, Greenwich, Conn. 314 pages. $27.50. Faces of Germany from 1910 to 1938.

PEOPLE
By Alfred Eisenstaedt. The Viking Press, New York. 264 pages. $17.95. A collection representing the work of one of the masters of photojournalism from the late 1920s to the early 1970s.

VICTORIAN PHOTOGRAPHS OF FAMOUS MEN AND FAIR WOMEN
By Julia Margaret Cameron. David R. Godine, Boston, Mass. Unnumbered pages. $20.00. The beautifully romantic work—portraits of a Victorian pioneer—is presented in an expanded and revised edition of a book originally published in 1926 by Leonard and Virginia Woolf.

EDWARD WESTON
Biography by Ben Maddow. Aperture Inc., Millerton, N.Y. 285 pages. $40.00. The definitive volume on the photographer noted for his meticulously detailed landscapes and nature studies.

THE WOMAN'S EYE
Edited by Anne Tucker. Alfred A. Knopf, New York. 170 pages. Hardbound, $15.00; softbound, $6.95. Selections from the work of women photographers of the past and present: Gertrude Kasebier, Frances Benjamin Johnston, Margaret Bourke-White, Dorothea Lange, Berenice Abbott, Barbara Morgan, Diane Arbus, Alisa Wells, Judy Dater and Bea Nattles.

Collections

THE LITERATURE OF PHOTOGRAPHY
Edited by Peter Bunnell and Robert A. Sobieszek. Arno Press, New York. A collection of reprints, facsimiles of the originals, of 62 books that constitute the original source material for the history of photography. Prices range from $4.50 to $30.00 for individual titles and the complete set is $903.00. Included are such classics as A. H. Wall's 1896 "Artistic Landscape Photography" ($11.00), H.P. Robinson's 1896 "The Elements of a Pictorial Photograph" ($11.00), Georges Potonniée's 1936 "The History of the Discovery of Photography" ($16.00), and Peter Henry Emerson's 1899 "Naturalistic Photography for Students of the Art" (3rd edition) and "The Death of Naturalistic Photography" (hardbound, $16.00; softbound, $4.95).

Technical

DARKROOM TECHNIQUES, VOL. 1 AND 2
By Andeas Feininger. Amphoto, Garden City, N.Y. $7.95 per volume, $15.00 for the set.

PHOTOGRAPHY, SOURCE AND RESOURCE
By Steven Lewis, James McQuaid and David Tait. Turnip Press, State College, Penn. (Distributed by Light Impressions, Rochester, N.Y.) 220 pages. $6.00. A compilation of basic data on university photographic education, workshops, publishing, critics, galleries and collections, and a bibliography of theses and dissertations.

SOLARIZATION
By Sandy Walker and Clarence Rainwater. Amphoto, Garden City, N.Y. 176 pages. $14.95. Techniques of controlling the partial reversal of tones produced by solarization.

THE ZONE VI WORKSHOP
By Fred Picker, Zone VI Studio, 147 Hill Air Circle, White Plains, N.Y. 10605. 134 pages. $5.95. Techniques for achieving a full-scale rendition of tones of gray in black-and-white prints.

The Major Shows

Little in the world of photography attracts as much attention during the year as the major exhibitions. Through them, talented photographers gain a rare opportunity to display their work for the appraisal of an art-conscious public. Some exhibitions serve broader purposes, giving photography perspective by reviewing the development of the medium. Of the scores of shows mounted around the world in 1973, three rested on this historical base. Although each was different, each helped clarify the role of photography in art. A Milwaukee display of the work of the inventive artist Man Ray revealed how he expanded the boundaries of photography in the 1920s, freeing it from the limitations of recording the natural world. Man Ray's innovations grew out of his experience as an avant-garde painter, yet painting itself owes much to photography, as was made plain at a small museum in Germany. There an ambitiously comprehensive exhibition traced the interdependence of these totally different ways of creating two-dimensional images. Finally, a New York show honoring the news photograph reminded viewers of a camera's elemental purpose—to convey ideas in unequivocal visual terms.

Eyes with Glass Beads, 1933

Sorrowing eyes secrete glass tears in an emotion-mocking close-up by Man Ray, whose iconoclastic approach—honored by an exhibition in 1973—foreshadowed techniques newly popular among avant-garde photographers.

71

Man Ray Rediscovered

Man Ray has long been a legendary figure in the history of modern art. As a leading member—and the only important American member—of the Dada and Surrealist movements that dominated the Paris avant-garde in the period between the two World Wars, he pursued an extraordinarily versatile career in painting, sculpture, collage, film making and still photography. Although art historians have rarely, if ever, overlooked Man Ray's photographs in attempting to assess his stature as an artist, they have nonetheless tended to base their judgments on his painting, a medium in which he has never produced really first-rate works. In 1973, however, the usual perspective was reversed in an exhibition organized by the Milwaukee Art Center and later shown at the Metropolitan Museum in New York: it provided the first comprehensive look at his photography, separated at last from his other endeavors. The result was a revelation. Seen strictly in his role as a photographer, Man Ray emerged as a far more original artist than many critics —and even his fellow Dadaists—had appreciated.

What was the nature of his photographic achievement? It must, I think, be seen as fundamentally divided between the poetry and the prose of the photographic medium. For Man Ray is, on the one hand, one of the pioneers of inventive photography, and, on the other, a superb practitioner of the straight picture. He has made photographs of what cannot be seen—pictures that can only be created in the photographic printing process—and he has also given us a dazzling series of portraits of his contemporaries. At times, too, we can see the creative effect of his experimental work on his more conventional pictures. He thus embraces the polarities by which the photographic medium is defined, and at the same time, a good deal of the space between them.

He began his career as a painter with no special interest in photography as an artistic medium. His first pictures were taken for a practical rather than an esthetic purpose: they were pictures of his own paintings. That was around 1915, the same year he met Marcel Duchamp, the Dada master who had a deeper influence on Man Ray's thinking—on his whole approach to art in any medium—than any other man.

They met in New York. Man Ray, then 25, was an unfocused American provincial of bohemian tastes, living in an artists' colony in New Jersey, showing his paintings for the first time, and still reeling from his encounter with the Armory Show two years earlier—the historic show that introduced the modern art of Europe to the American public. Duchamp, only three years older, was already a notorious symbol of the French avant-garde and the most talked-about painter in the Armory Show (his work excited the wrath of no less a figure than Teddy Roosevelt). Even then he was in the process of abandoning painting for more esoteric, antiart escapades.

The author of this article, Hilton Kramer, is art news editor of *The New York Times* and one of the nation's most respected art critics. His recent book, *The Age of Avant-Garde,* is a selection of his essays and reviews.

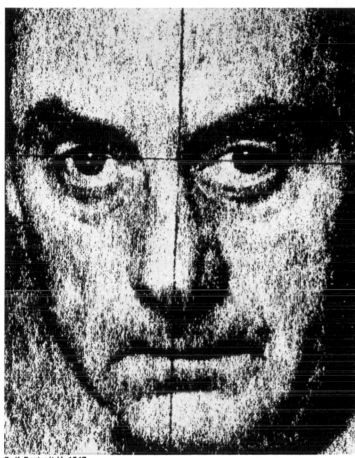
Self-Portrait V, 1947

Man Ray's self-portrait, made comparatively late
in his career from a zinc-plate photoengraving
of a photograph, bears etched perpendicular
lines that could be a suggestion of a drafting
exercise, a rifle's telescopic sight—or a
purely arbitrary touch. Ray refuses to explain.

In New York, in the midst of a war that much of the avant-garde intelligentsia on both sides of the Atlantic mocked and despised, Duchamp was launching his own branch of the Dada movement, promulgating a systematic disrespect for traditional conceptions of high culture and elevating machine-made commercial objects to a position of esthetic superiority over the conventional productions of the fine arts, which were declared obsolete. Man Ray became an instant convert to this Dada ideology, and the course of his later work was set.

Like Man Ray in this early period, Duchamp too had no interest in photography as an art. He looked upon it merely as a handy weapon in his war against the pretensions of painting. His only statement on the matter occurred in a 1922 letter to Alfred Stieglitz, the leader of the Photo-Secession movement: "You know exactly how I feel about photography. I would like to see it make people despise painting until something else will make photography unbearable." But this essentially negative attitude had an unintended positive effect on the work of his devoted American disciple. It liberated Man Ray from conventional expectations about art in any medium, and it thus allowed him to approach photography with an inspired freedom and energy.

In 1921, Man Ray left New York for Paris, to which Duchamp had already returned. There, the aspiring American avant-gardist took up photography again—initially for the pragmatic purpose of earning a living. Through the wife of an artist-friend, Ray was introduced to Paul Poiret, at that time a reigning mandarin of the French fashion world. Poiret invited him to try his hand at fashion photography. It was in the process of developing his first prints for this commisson, working in a makeshift darkroom in his cheap hotel room—so the often-quoted story goes—that the first Rayographs were created. This is the way Man Ray described the event in his memoirs:

"One sheet of photo paper got into the developing tray—a sheet unexposed that had been mixed with those already exposed under the negatives . . . and as I waited in vain a couple of minutes for an image to appear, regretting the waste of paper, I mechanically placed a small glass funnel, the graduate and the thermometer in the tray on the wetted paper. I turned on the light; before my eyes an image began to form, not quite a simple silhouette of the objects as in a straight photograph, but distorted and refracted by the glass more or less in contact with the paper and standing out against a black background, the part directly exposed to the light. . . . I made a few more prints, setting aside the more serious work for Poiret, using up my precious paper. Taking whatever objects came to hand; my hotel-room key, a handkerchief, some pencils, a brush, a candle, a piece of twine—it wasn't necessary to put them in the liquid but on the dry paper

73

first, exposing it to the light for a few seconds as with the negatives—I made a few more prints, excitedly, enjoying myself immensely. In the morning I examined the results, pinning a couple of Rayographs—as I decided to call them—on the wall. They looked startlingly new and mysterious."

Whether we take this as an actual account of Man Ray's creation of his first cameraless photographs or as only another of his Dada inventions (we know, of course, that the German Dadaist, Christian Schad, had already produced similar works four years earlier) is less important than the fact that something truly significant was achieved. To exploit the accidental and to apotheosize the workings of chance were the very essence of the Dada mystique. And chance, in this case, had opened up a whole new world.

In the Rayographs, photography was liberated from the "reality" of observed appearances and won the power to create its subjects as freely as the most visionary poetry. Indeed, it was in his Rayographs that Man Ray most closely approximated the subjective freedom of the Surrealist poets. The camera, which he continued to use with great distinction, was dislodged as a creative necessity and became instead what it has ever since remained: a technical and stylistic option.

Ray continued to exercise the option both ways. At one extreme he produced pictures that are highly improvisatory and manipulated, specializing in those free-form juxtapositions of objects transmuted into abstractions that are the special glory of the Dada sensibility. At the other, he photographed some of the most celebrated artists and writers of the century with affectionate, documentary clarity.

Occasionally, too, Man Ray applied some of the visual lessons of the Rayographs to his straight pictures and to his solarized prints, adding details of pure invention to real-life subjects—as in his *Eyes with Glass Beads (page 71)* or his self-portrait *(page 73).* For the most part, however, Man Ray has kept the poetry and the prose of his photographic work separate enterprises, bringing excellence to each. The 1973 exhibition, drawn from the great private collection of Arnold H. Crane, leaves no room for any doubt that Man Ray's works belong among the classics of photography—the field in which he ceased to be an amiable disciple and became instead an innovator and master in his own right. *Hilton Kramer* □

Wasp, Date unknown

Injecting nightmare into a coastal landscape,
Ray placed a wasp on the negative when he
made this print. "I like contradictions," said
Ray. "We have never obtained the infinite
variety and contradictions that exist in nature.".

Reclining Nude, 1929

A nude's flesh seems to melt into the carpet in an eerie image produced by solarization. When developing the negative, Ray flashed a light on it; the brief secondary exposure caused a partial reversal of tones, transforming what had been the glare of a spotlight on the model's left side into a gray extension of her body.

The sculptured quality of a still life of lilies was also achieved by solarization during development. In addition to altering the tones, the technique forms dark, sharply defined lines at the boundaries between highlight and shadow areas.

Solarized Lilies, 1931

Rayograph, 1927

Created without a camera, this cryptic shadow picture was made by placing objects directly on a piece of photographic paper and then exposing the paper to light before developing.

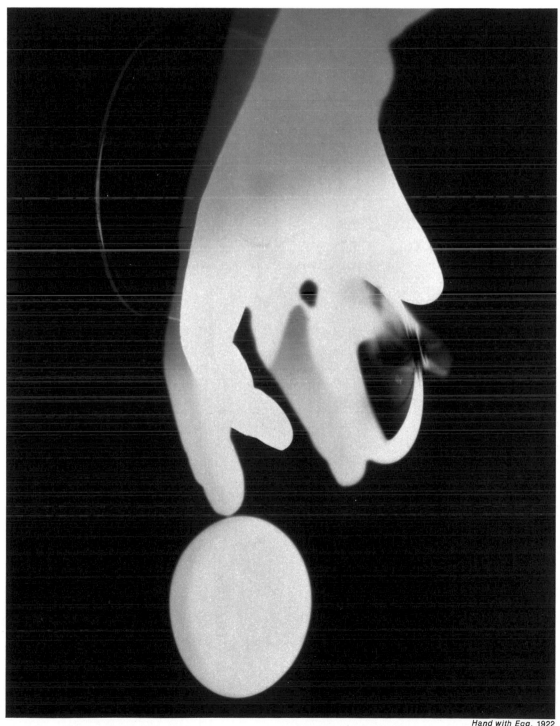

In another shadow picture, the shapes of a hand and egg are clear, yet their meaning remains elusive. Ray double-exposed the photographic paper to show the hand first holding and then releasing the egg. Ray was typically perverse when discussing such images, which he immodestly called Rayographs: "They are the result of curiosity, inspiration, and these words do not intend to convey any information."

Hand with Egg, 1922

Barbette, 1926

Ray made a montage portrait of a French transvestite acrobat named Barbette (left) by sandwiching two negatives to show the star, dressed in female costume, performing on the high wire behind his heavily made-up image.

Paul Chadourne (right), a companion to Ray in ▶ the scoffing, nihilistic art movement called Dada, is the image of the dashing bourgeois—except that his driving goggles have been strangely mutilated in the photographer's darkroom.

Chadourne, 1928

Lens and Brush: A Stormy Liaison

A visitor to the exhibition entitled "With Camera, Paint Brush and Spray Gun," held last summer in the small West German town of Recklinghausen, could be pardoned a moment of confusion. The show included both paintings and photographs, but at first glance the visitor might not know which was which. The photographs looked like photographs, all right, but so did most of the paintings. They were all either based on photographs or painted to look as much like photographs as possible.

The heart of the show was a large group of works by Photo-Realist painters, the newest school to achieve an international reputation. These paintings not only looked like photographs—they were, in fact, largely hand-painted enlargements of photographs, and many visitors, brought up on the modernist dogma that copying photographs is the greatest sin in painting, may have wondered why they were in an art museum. The Recklinghausen exhibition answered this question by furnishing Photo-Realism with a respectable ancestry in art history.

Like any exhibition designed to prove a point, the Recklinghausen show left out a lot. It concentrated on realistic styles, and even within the realist tradition it omitted some classic examples. Nevertheless, this show said something new by linking the explicit use of photography today with its widespread but often furtive use in the past. In the process it provided an eye-opening account of the tangled relations between painting and photography since photography was introduced in 1839.

The stormy liaison is as old as photography itself. Photography was at first generally accepted as completely equal to painting except for its disappointing lack of color. "Mr. Daguerre's process completely satisfies art's every need," wrote the popular painter Paul Delaroche in a report to a committee of the French Academy. "It carries some of art's basic qualities to such perfection that it will become for even the most skillful painters a subject for observation and study. The painter will find this technique a rapid way of making collections of studies that he could otherwise obtain only with much time and trouble, and, whatever his talents might be, in a far less perfect manner. When this technique becomes known, the publication of inexact views will no longer be tolerated."

Photography's ability to record nature was so evident to painters and public alike that many painters feared its competition. "This is the end of Art, I am glad I have had my day," said the English landscape painter J.M.W. Turner. According to a persistent tradition, Delaroche himself was so frightened by his first view of a daguerreotype that he ran about Paris exclaiming, "From this day, painting is dead."

Of course, painting did not die. However, as Delaroche predicted, painters as great as Turner and Delacroix began to study photographs while less-

Gene Thornton, the author of this article, is a photography critic for *The New York Times* and a contributing editor to *Art News*. He studied art in New York and is currently writing and lecturing on painting and photography.

GEORGE HENDRIK BREITNER: *The Red Kimono*, 1893

To create the oil painting above, 19th Century Dutch artist George Hendrik Breitner first took the photograph opposite. He used the photograph in place of a preliminary sketch, painting from it, but using color and minor changes in shape to soften the realism and produce a stylized portrait typical of the period.

er painters took to copying them wholesale *(left)*. Within 20 years of photography's invention, the practice of copying from photographs was so widespread the French critic Theophile Gautier caustically suggested that the Paris Salon award a special medal to the daguerreotype as the unacknowledged collaborator in so many painters' work.

While photography aided some painters more than they cared to admit, it took work away from others. By the 1850s most portraits and topographical views of landscape and buildings were being done by photographers. These two specialties had been the bread-and-butter work of innumerable painters and draftsmen and, when they were taken over by photography, painters began to question whether photography could be art. Increasingly they wanted to confine it to a subsidiary role as a humble recorder of facts. "If photography is allowed to encroach on the domain of the impalpable and the imaginary, upon anything whose value depends solely upon the addition of some things of a man's soul, then it will be so much the worse for us." So wrote the poet and critic Charles Baudelaire in his review of the Paris Salon of 1859, and his view was widely shared.

Obviously this new attitude toward photography was based in part on professional jealousy. Painters were afraid of being replaced by cameras. But in part it was also based on a changed view of art. Everyone conceded that photography was quicker and cheaper than painting and in many ways superior to painting when it came to a realistic representation of nature. However, the question arose whether realistic representation was the whole of art, whether indeed anything that a machine like a camera did so well could be art. The general feeling was that it could not, and critics began to encourage painters to concentrate on those aspects of art that were held to be beyond the reach of a machine: on pure form, color and very personalized expression. Photographic realism and objectivity came to be terms of abuse in art criticism, and painters as diverse as Whistler and Gauguin began to pride themselves on being as unphotographic as possible.

The trend away from realism did not stop most painters from using photography. Even avant-garde painters worked from photographs, though the distortions they introduced into their paintings usually concealed the fact, while other artists used them freely. Then as now, the public loved realistic detail in its pictures, and photography helped painters achieve a more accurate representation, particularly of action and movement *(page 85)*. It also provided inspiration for many designs and motifs. However, the use of photography became a dirty little secret, almost like sex in Victorian England, and painters tried harder than ever to conceal their connection with it.

There were also photographers who began to be ashamed of the easy realism that had been characteristic of their medium. Mid-Victorian photographers softened and sentimentalized their sitters or tried to re-create the stagy effects of then-popular painting styles. At the end of the 19th Century, art photographers started to imitate the hazy, tonal effects of Whistler and the Impressionists. Later still, when abstract painting came into vogue, artists like Man Ray showed how abstract effects might be achieved by photographic means. But most photography concerned itself with straightforward record-making and documentation, while painting turned its back on objectivity in a search for ever-more-personal expression in increasingly idiosyncratic styles.

This neat and handy division of labor was never securely founded. Too many painters and draftsmen never advanced beyond routine representation, while too many photographers went way beyond it. However, it was not until the 1970s that the division was violently upset by the rise of the Photo-Realists, a whole school of painters whose visible aim was to be as photographic as possible. Despite recent books and exhibitions that had conclusively demonstrated the use of photography by painters in the past, most viewers were unprepared for such unabashed copying. The older painters had used photography sparingly, hesitantly and often secretly, but the new Photo-Realists used it shamelessly, openly, blatantly. They clearly aimed not merely to work from photographs but to reproduce the tone, feel and texture of the photographic print, and they worked from the kind of banal photographs that are furthest removed from traditional ideas of art: family snapshots, photomat portraits, postcards, advertisements, pinup nudes and news photographs.

Critics differ about the value of the results. Some hail Photo-Realism as a revolutionary and exciting new way of calling attention to the texture of modern life, while others feel that its bland neutrality and lack of explicit comment make it deeply conservative. Some welcome it as a return to subject matter after the long rule of abstraction, while others damn it as a gimmick worth no more than abstract gimmicks that preceded it.

It is too early to say which if any of these views is correct, but one thing is already clear: Photo-Realist painting could not come into being before photography had become an intimate part of everyone's daily life. Whatever its value, it is certainly a tribute to the omnipresence of photography in modern life. It is also something new in the long and stormy relationship of painting to photography. As the Recklinghausen survey shows, Photo-Realist painting has roots in the past, but the open dominance of photographic imagery in these paintings is without precedent. Pessimists might see it as the death of the individual vision in the one pictorial art where it has been incontestably present, but optimists might see it as a triumph of Photo Lib on the enemy's own turf.

Gene Thornton □

Early photographs like these, created by placing ▶ objects on light-sensitive paper and then exposing them to sunlight, were widely praised as a new art form by contemporaries. In England, William Henry Fox Talbot coined the term photogenic drawing to describe his work, including the lace embroidery pattern at top left. In France, Hippolyte Bayard produced images of pressed flowers and leaves, top right.

An early experimenter in multiple-exposure ▶ photography, American artist Thomas Eakins took pictures like the one at bottom to help him paint bodies in motion. Disks fastened to the running man make it easier to follow movements of ankle, knee, hip, shoulder and head.

WILLIAM HENRY FOX TALBOT: *Lace*, 1842

HIPPOLYTE BAYARD: *Pressed Plants*, 1839

THOMAS EAKINS: *Marey Wheel Photograph of Jesse Godley*, 1884

Photography and painting blend in a collage
made in the 1920s. Cutout photographs, mounted
on a painted background and rephotographed,
produced this cryptically titled abstraction.

LÁSZLÓ MOHOLY-NAGY: *The Girls' Boarding School*, 1925

A variation of the collage technique is shown in this photomontage. Parts of three photographs create an expression of alienation in a big city —possibly the artist in the Berlin of the '30s.

HERBERT BAYER: *Lonely Native of a Big City,* 1932

The two commercial photographs below, taken from magazines, were models for the painting at right. The artist, a leader of the Photo-Realists, whose paintings emulate photographs, used the pictures to simulate ripped billboard posters.

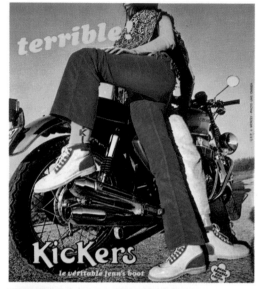

FRITZ KÖTHE: *Kickers,* 1971

A painting of a theater marquee, copied from a projected color slide, typifies the attentiveness to detail of the Photo-Realist approach. The artist has added a bit of irony to his cliché theme by including the neoned word "art"

ROBERT COTTINGHAM: *Art*, 1971

89

ROBERT BECHTLE: '62 Chevy, 1970

*This startlingly authentic rendering of a parked
car is the result of an attempt to reproduce in oils
the photographic product of a candid camera.
It is copied from a slide projected onto canvas.*

*A tinted etching of a news photograph showing a
crowded city square is overlaid with a series of
cryptic lines and symbols, apparently to indicate
the artist's personal involvement in his work.*

PRAVOSLAV SOVÁK: *Place*, 1969-1970

CHUCK CLOSE: *Keith*, 1969-1970

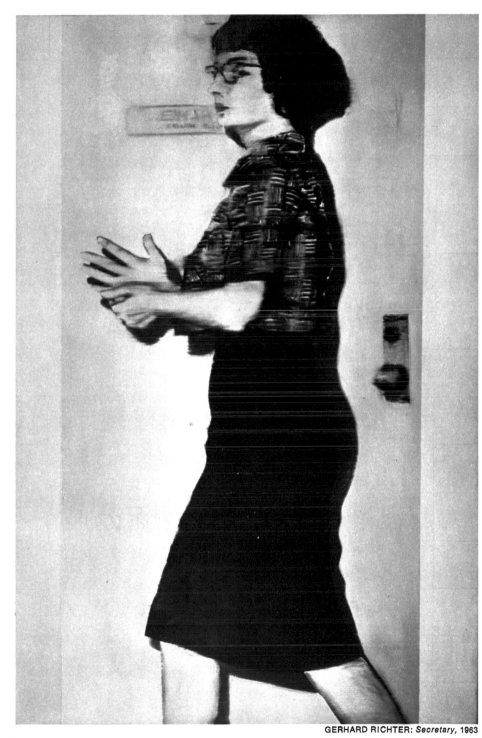

◄ This "facescape"—the original is 9 x 7 feet—is one of a black-and-white series painted from 11 x 14-inch photographs of the artist's friends. It took him two months, working section by section with airbrush and razor blade, to match the tiniest details of hair and complexion.

This slightly blurred version of a flash-bulb-lit news photograph was painted life size. The artist, fascinated by the photograph's many shades of gray, created his unusual study by applying oils over a sketch, then smoothing the brush marks.

GERHARD RICHTER: *Secretary*, 1963

Homage to the News Picture

When we think of great news pictures, the examples that immediately come to mind are exciting glimpses of intense action—the fiery death of the zeppelin *Hindenburg,* Presidential assassin Lee Harvey Oswald being fatally shot in a crowded Dallas police station, a burned and naked Vietnamese girl fleeing from her bombed village *(page 185).*

But such prize-winning pictures, while undeniably memorable, fail to show the news photographer's real talent. They are in large part lucky accidents, products of good fortune that, perhaps just once in a lifetime, place photographer and camera where an unexpected—and strikingly visual—event is about to take place. The vast majority of news pictures involve no such luck. Instead, they record events of fleeting importance—a political rally, a beauty contest, a murder, a prize fight—that fill the daily assignment sheet. The story, no matter how banal, must be made to catch a hurrying reader's attention, and more important, it must be told completely in a single picture. Telling a story—any story—in one picture is the expert news photographer's real achievement. Behind it lie skills and techniques fundamental to all photography but little appreciated until a sensitively assembled show, "From the Picture Press," was presented at New York's Museum of Modern Art in January 1973. As the museum's first such exhibition devoted exclusively to news photography craftsmanship, it opened the eyes of both critics and public to a familiar but poorly understood branch of photography.

The pictures the museum displayed, some nearly half a century old, seem routine, like any number of others that might appear today or tomorrow. They are simple, direct views of familiar subjects. Only after looking at them and then away does the viewer realize that a quick glimpse of the photograph has told him practically everything he needed to know about the event—a realization emphasized by the absence of written captions, which the museum grouped apart from the pictures, as they are at the end of this section *(page 104).* It was a dramatic way of proving that a good news picture needs no words to convey its basic message.

Such eye-stopping, informative pictures of everyday news events attest to the news photographer's craftsmanship, for he generally works under severe handicaps. Unlike other photographers, he has little control over his subjects and working conditions. His job is to take his assigned pictures quickly with whatever equipment he has on hand. He cannot spend time laboring over the esthetic effects of light and shadows or the subtleties of composition—such touches would largely be lost in any case by harsh reproduction on newsprint. Nor can he afford the photojournalist's luxury of shooting a sequence of pictures that spell out an event.

To compound his problem, the news photographer is often called upon to record an event that has already occurred. Most spot-news pictures fall into

WEEGEE (ARTHUR FELLIG), 1941

The presence of a news photographer in this deceptively serene scene tells the reader that despite the seeming disinterest of police and passersby, the man in the car is dead.

this category, and the news photographer must use all of his inventiveness to come up with a picture that gives the message without actually showing the event itself. He succeeds by combining the skillful application of basic photographic techniques—camera angle and framing—with easily recognized visual symbols to create a picture whose message is as unmistakable as a newspaper headline.

It is the use of symbols to make a picture tell a complete story that distinguishes expert news photography—as is made plain by the samples in the show. These symbols become a kind of language, images that the photographer can manipulate to convey often complex ideas. If the message is that a murder has just taken place, the most effective way to convey it is to show the victim at the scene of the crime or, as in the example on this page, where he was found by the police. Oldtime news photographers were not above reconstructing a murder scene with the help of friendly policemen. But even when reconstruction is not possible—or, in the case of a gruesome murder, desirable—the photographer can use specialized gestures or poses to convey his meaning. A viewer recognizes instantly that the man shielding his face from the camera is a villain, while the smiling man holding hands clasped over his head is a victor. A picture of a woman slumped beside the desk of an emotionless detective, an empty revolver in the foreground, says that a murderess has confessed. The expressions on the faces of two boys staring down at whatever has been revealed by the hand of a detective lifting a sheet tells the newspaper reader only too clearly what is under the sheet. One of the most moving pictures in the exhibition is a close-up of a man holding a little girl's shoes and socks—and a length of clothesline knotted into a noose. In the signpost-strewn world of news photography, happy people are always shown laughing or smiling, unhappy people are always shown crying or frowning.

Such symbols easily become clichés. Yet they are basic to the purpose of any photograph—the transmission of an idea by means of a visual pattern —and they are employed in one transmutation or another by all serious photographers. In some cases this use of the news photograph's language is obvious, as it is in the work of the late Diane Arbus (who before her death helped plan the museum show). She deliberately adapted newspaper symbolism, sometimes making a wry point by including props such as toys or pets in her poignant character studies. In other cases the visual language is much more subtle, and simply to identify its elements requires some careful study. There actually may be no symbols as such. Instead, facial expression, bodily pose and shadow placement may become the elements the news photographer skillfully manipulates to tell his story, whatever it may be. The captions supply only the details.

Ceremonies

RICHARD CORKERY, 1968

Because these pictures were selected as outstanding examples of the news photographer's ability to tell a story without words, they are shown separate from the captions, which are on page 104.

Contests

CHARLES HOFF, 1959

Winners

PHOTOGRAPHER UNKNOWN, 1952

Losers

Disasters

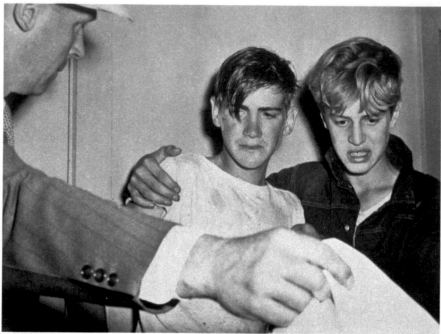

TED NEEDHAM, 1947

PHOTOGRAPHER UNKNOWN, 1937

DICK PEARE, date unknown

Good News...

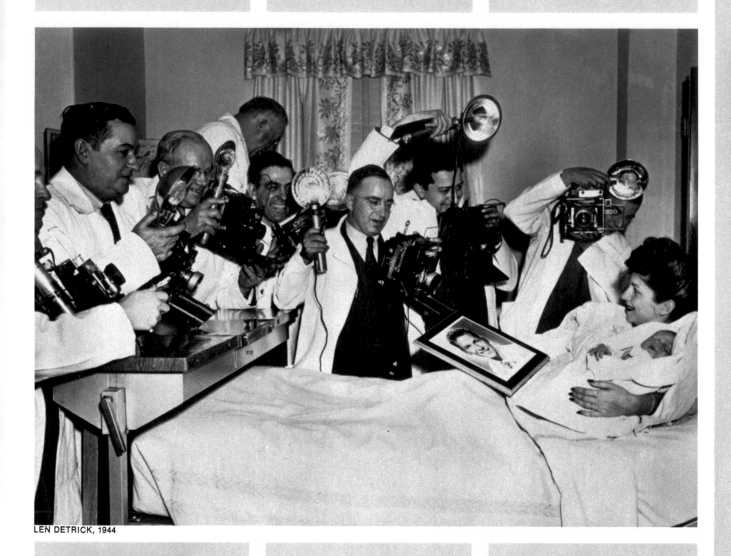

LEN DETRICK, 1944

and the Good Life

PHOTOGRAPHER UNKNOWN, 1936

103

Happily joining hands at a 1968 Republican rally in Madison Square Garden are, left to right, Spiro Agnew, Richard Nixon, George Romney and Nelson Rockefeller.

Stricken champion Floyd Patterson rises from the first of seven third-round knockdowns by champion-to-be Ingemar Johansson at Yankee Stadium in 1959.

Typical of the publicity setups that all news photographers must cope with is this one of a bikinied 1952 Frankfurter Queen in a sausage maker's "throne room."

In a police headquarters scene dating from around 1950, a woman collapses after telling a Pittsburgh detective how she killed her father with the gun on the table.

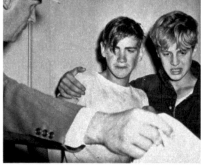

Harold Reed, left, and Donald Horn fight back tears as they prepare to identify the body of their friend, 12-year-old Donald Goudie, shot by a Queens junkman in 1947.

A Brooklyn detective holds the items found on the body of eight-year-old Paula Magagna, murdered in 1937: her shoes, socks and the rope used to strangle her.

The death of this man, lying as police found him, was news when it was recorded in the 1930s, but the details of name and place are now lost from the files.

Mrs. Frank Sinatra shows off the singer's newborn son, Frank Jr., in 1944 to a horde of photographers who descended upon Jersey City's Margaret Hague Hospital.

As the last moments of 1935 tick away, New Year's Eve partygoers prepare to toast the arrival of 1936 from the crowded bar of Manhattan's St. Moritz Hotel.

Discoveries

Although the number of serious photographers in America, Europe and Asia grows each year, only a few win recognition for their distinctive achievements. All too often, their reward is limited to local exhibitions of their work and the acclaim of a handful of appreciative critics. It is to seek out the best of these newly discovered talents and to introduce them to a widespread audience that PHOTOGRAPHY YEAR undertakes an annual international search. A panel of consultants, selected both for their knowledge of new photographers and for their own photographic expertise, submitted a list of 50 nominees for this issue. From this gifted group the Editors have selected four (opposite) whose work—described and illustrated on pages 110-140—promises to attract more and more attention in years to come.

MARCIA RESNICK

CLAUDINE GUÉNIOT

JOSEPH JACHNA

TERRY WILD

107

Discovering the Discoveries

How is a "discovery" discovered? The four photographers whose work is exhibited on the following pages were selected by a painstaking process that began in August 1973 when the Editors of PHOTOGRAPHY YEAR chose a panel of six consultants. Each is an authority in a region rich in photographic talent and activity. The consultants were asked to prepare a list of gifted new photographers whose work had come to their attention during the previous year. The age, sex and background of the photographer were to be irrelevant, and the consultants were instructed to consider every style, technique and subject matter, no matter how familiar or how unconventional. While the photographs were expected to be of professional quality, the photographers had to be relatively unrecognized in the field. Excluded from consideration were photographers making a full-time living from their work, as well as those whose pictures had already received prominence in books, exhibitions or museum collections. The consultants screened scores of candidates in arriving at a list of 50 nominees, drawn from nine nations and three continents. From this list, the Editors selected the four finalists —each one of them a distinctive talent whose work seems certain to become widely known in years to come.

Joseph Jachna *(pages 110-117)* is a Chicago photography instructor who, at 38, is the oldest of the newcomers. A master of photographic illusion, he turns nature into something altogether new and mystifying by welding his own hands and arms to the surrounding world. Claudine Guéniot *(pages 118-125)* is a young Parisienne whose haunting woodland and mountain scenes mark her as a photographer of unusual technical skill and sensitivity. Terry Wild *(pages 126-133)* is a 27-year-old Pennsylvanian who documents a peculiarly 20th Century American landscape—open space almost featureless except for a car or highway. Marcia Resnick *(pages 134-140),* youngest of the quartet at 23, is a native of Brooklyn who studied photography in California. She creates very personal pictures from routine black-and-white snapshots of ordinary people in ordinary situations, converting these artless scenes into startling disjunctures with reality by painting the people in cheery colors while leaving their surroundings untouched.

THE PHOTOGRAPHY YEAR
Panel of Consultants

Top row, left to right

JEAN-CLAUDE LEMAGNY
Curator of Contemporary Photographs, Cabinet des
Estampes, Bibliothèque Nationale, Paris

SHOJI YAMAGISHI
Editor, *Camera Mainichi*, Tokyo

FREDERICK SOMMER
Photographer and teacher, former Coordinator of Fine
Arts Studies, Prescott College, Prescott, Arizona

Bottom row, left to right

FRED R. PARKER
Executive Director, Friends of Photography, Carmel,
California

SUE DAVIES
Director, The Photographers' Gallery, London

DANIELA MRÁZKOVÁ
Editor, *Fotografie*, Prague

Photographers Nominated by the Consultants

BILL ARNOLD, *Florence, Massachusetts*
RYOJI AKIYAMA, *Tokyo*
DAVID AVISON, *Chicago*
HELENA BAIERLE, *Prague*
RICHARD BARTLETT, *North Kingstown, R.I.*
JEAN CHARLES BATS, *Chatillon, France*
LOUIS BERNAL, *Tucson*
MAUREEN BISILLIAT, *São Paulo, Brazil*
THOMAS BROWN, *New Haven, Connecticut*
TOM DRAHOS, *Paris*
JAKUB RUDOLF DUDA, *Prague*
JAY DUSARD, *Kirkland, Arizona*
MARK EDWARDS, *London*
REED ESTABROOK, *Tolono, Illinois*
JEAN FOREST, *Paris*
FRANÇOISE, *Paris*
DICK FRANK, *New York City*
JILL FREEDMAN, *New York City*
*CLAUDINE GUÉNIOT, *Paris*
ANTHONY HERNANDEZ, *Los Angeles*
WERNER HIEBEL, *Garching, West Germany*
PAUL HILL, *Wolverhampton, England*
JOSEF HNÍK, *Prague*
MIROSLAV HUCEK, *Prague*
*JOSEPH JACHNA, *Oak Lawn, Illinois*

BISHIN JUMONJI, *Tokyo*
JOSEF KOUDELKA, *London*
MICHEL KRZYZANOWSKI, *Den Bosch, Netherlands*
ELLEN LANDWEBER, *Culver City, California*
MARKETA LUSKACOVA, *Prague*
ALEXANDRAS MACIAUSKAS, *Kaunas, USSR*
RON McCORMICK, *London*
JEAN FRANÇOIS MALAMOUD, *Bourges, France*
MARGITA MANCOVÁ, *Bratislava, Czechoslovakia*
FRANTIŠEK MARŠALEK, *Brno, Czechoslovakia*
DETLEF ORLOPP, *Kempen, West Germany*
*MARCIA RESNICK, *New York City*
FRANÇOISE SAUR, *Colmar, France*
PETR SIKULA, *Ostrava, Czechoslovakia*
KEITH SMITH, *Chicago*
CHARLES SPINK, *Santa Paula, California*
PAVEL ŠTECHA, *Prague*
ISSEI SUDA, *Tokyo*
JEAN-LUC TARTARIN, *Vandelainville, France*
LEWIS THOMAS, *San Francisco*
HIROMI TSUCHIDA, *Tokyo*
KATSUMI WATANABE, *Tokyo*
*TERRY WILD, *Williamsport, Pennsylvania*
DINA WOELFFER, *Los Angeles*
KOHEI YOSHIYUKI, *Tokyo*

*Work of these photographers is shown on the following pages.

Joseph Jachna: Landscape Illusions

The extraordinary landscapes on the following pages might be said to represent a country called Joseph Jachna. In every one of these pictures, the fingers, hand or arm of the photographer are clearly visible, often the most conspicuous single element in the picture. But the identity of human flesh is obscured: the photographer has become a part of the landscape.

Here is a world of fingers (or are they megaliths?) that stretch to the sky; of arms (if indeed they are arms and not ancient rock formations) long enough to reach to the horizon; of mountains (hands?) that loom high overhead; of stones or ribbons of concrete that float and dance in a hand-held circlet of light. It is a puzzling, exciting, enchanted world that seems to defy the laws of physics—a world of illusion that is reproduced with all the clear and undoubted veracity that photography can muster.

Jachna studied at the Institute of Design in Chicago and has worked in commercial photography. At age 38, he has a number of exhibitions and publications behind him, but these surrealistic landscapes represent a new departure. He began the series when he was teaching a summer workshop class in Door County, Wisconsin. He had bought a wide-angle lens several years earlier but had never used it. Now he put it on his single-lens reflex camera and looked through the viewfinder. His own hand was sticking into the picture, and he suddenly realized that it looked like a monstrous rock formation. He turned and twisted his hand into various relations with the surrounding landscape; it became a windswept ridge, the barkless trunk of a fallen tree, a petrified bone. Later he discovered that he could compound the play of shifting and intermingling identities by holding a mirror or magnifying glass in his hand.

Jachna describes these images as "concise observations from life, very much distilled and simplified in form"—and he likes to compare them to poetry. But perhaps no analogy can quite do them justice. Jachna's artistry works on its own terms, and it is deeply satisfying—for even after the viewer has figured out the visual trick used to create the pictures, the mystery remains.

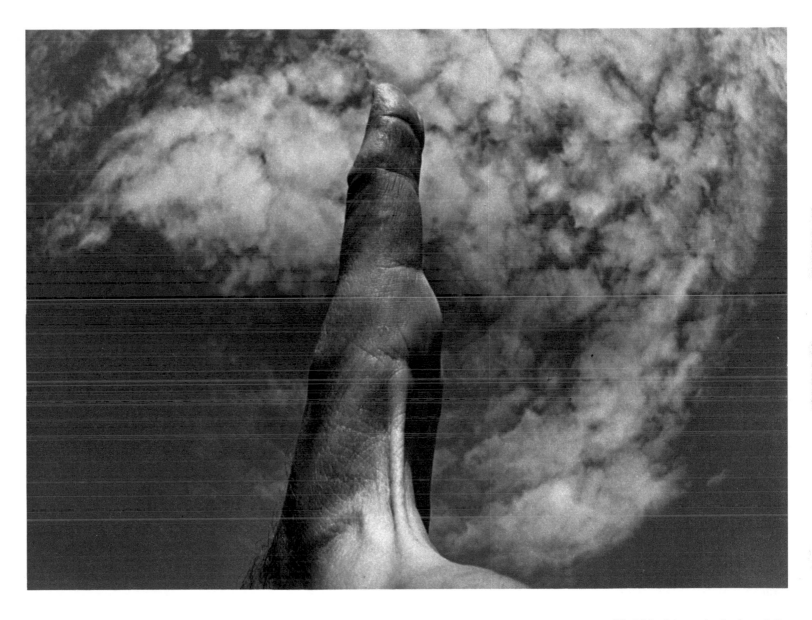

What this picture actually shows is the photographer's index finger radically foreshortened by a wide-angle lens. What it seems to show is a fractured and wind-eroded tower of rock that stretches into the clouds.

Out of a seam in the pebbly surface of an oddly
bulging road, finger-like shapes seem to grow in
two directions. So clever is the illusion that it is
almost impossible to tell what is real and what
is merely a reflection in the small, rectangular
mirror the photographer holds in one hand.

A stately, full-rigged ship seems to be floating over the grass of a sunlit meadow toward a shore of concrete debris. A closer look turns the sails into fingers and shows that half the landscape is really the other half reflected in a mirror.

The photographer's arm stretches down one side of a road to the horizon, where it meets the other side of the road at the vanishing point. This unusual perspective is caused by two lenses: the camera's wide-angle lens and a small rectangular lens held in the photographer's hand.

A gigantic, partly blackened, bonelike shape lying
in the grass is in fact the photographer's forearm,
which appears in another guise—this time
strangely withered—in Jachna's elongated shadow.

*A circular shaving mirror held in one hand
extends the rugged surface of a sunlit stone wall
into an area where shadows should be. In this
incongruous space, the photographer's fingers and
their reflections form a stack of dark holes.*

An enormous, menacing heap of rocks seems to be heaving its bulk up into the sky. But a second look reveals the heaped pile as the photographer's hand stretching away in the exaggerated perspective of the wide-angle lens.

Claudine Guéniot: The Soul of Nature

Claudine Guéniot's photographs of trees, leaves and rocks have a force and shimmering beauty that seem to stem directly from the 19th Century landscape art of her native France. Yet the pictures are deeply personal, representing this young woman's own photographic search for the essentials in nature—"the souls of rocks and leaves," she says. They are not so much portraits of specific places as they are landscapes of the artist's own sensibility. Really, she is looking for herself in everything she photographs. "Nature is only a pretext," she says. "If I am in front of something that is so beautiful it does not need my interpretation, I do not take the picture."

On the one hand, there is the shy and private person of the woodland scenes, fleeing the bustle of the city for a sylvan countryside. On the other hand, there is the strong woman in a desert of stony spikes. And somewhere in between is the mystic who can find solace, or perhaps even salvation, by concentrating on the fragile forms of a bank of leaves or fern fronds. No wonder Guéniot is made nervous by the thought of a showing of her work. "When I have an exhibition, my self-conscious and my subconscious are laid bare."

These evocations of the souls in nature—and her own emotional terrain —are created by a variety of photographic techniques. She achieves the aura of her woodland scenes by photographing them through the ruled transparent screen that photoengravers use—it deflects light waves to create a light-struck effect.

Another technique produces the silvery hairline around her leaf and rock forms. It is the result of the partial reversal of tones caused when the print is flashed with light, or solarized, during development. Sometimes she tones her prints with special chemicals to achieve the rich chestnut brown or delicate sepia often used in 19th Century photographs, and sometimes she leaves them starkly black and white.

All of Guéniot's photographs—even the most forceful among them—display a subtlety of tone and an intricate delicacy that is distinctly her own. Though she is now only 30 years old and her pictures have not previously been published or exhibited in America, her work has been included in shows in Europe since 1968.

The light that fills this forest in Burgundy blends tree trunks, leaves and air with a seamless, glowing translucency.

Each leaf of this bramble patch in a Burgundy forest is a world in itself, singled out for examination alone and yet an element contributing to a greater whole.

In another part of the forest, ferns push
through brambles, forming a silvery shower
of tracery against a chestnut ground.

In the French Alps, Guéniot found this
towering rock formation, one of several
she photographed for a proposed book,
"Stones of Hell." Against a black
sky, it seems endowed with inner light.

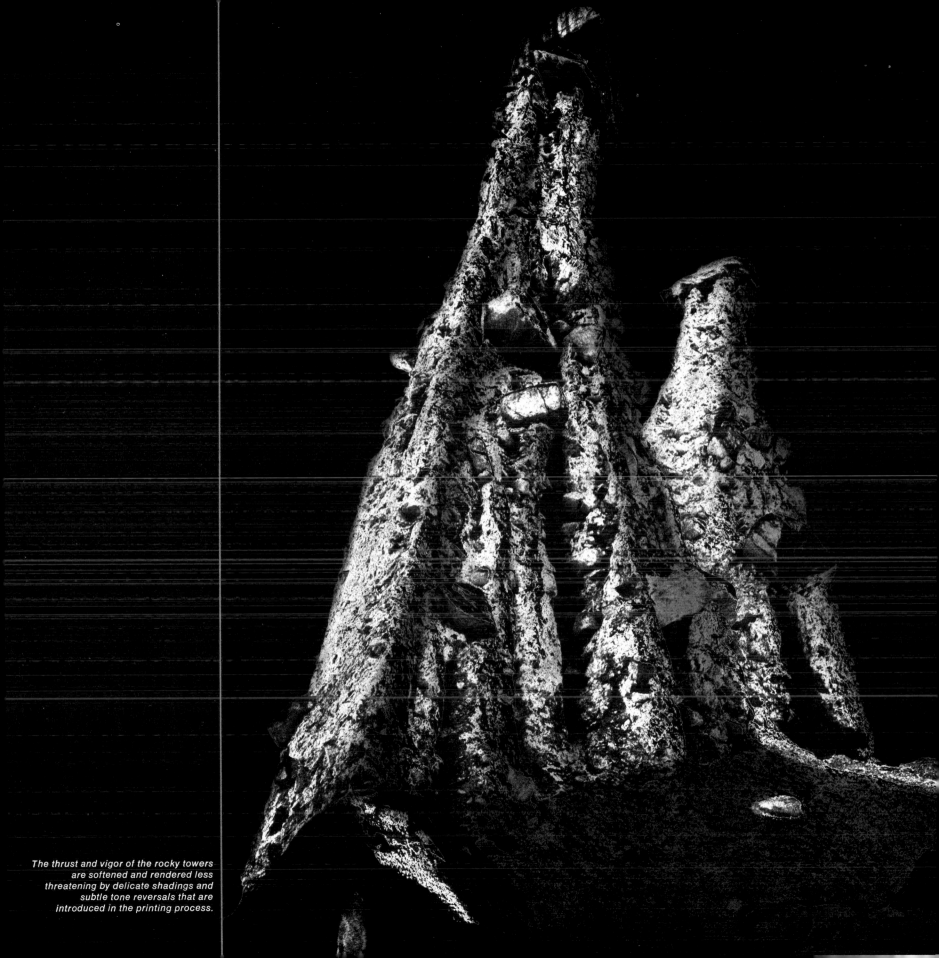

The thrust and vigor of the rocky towers are softened and rendered less threatening by delicate shadings and subtle tone reversals that are introduced in the printing process.

In a sunny, serene glade, a woodpile appears to belong as much to the forest as it does to any human.

Where this rutted lane actually leads remains a deliberate mystery; in the photographer's mind the path seems headed into a state of luminous glory.

Terry Wild: Empty World of the Road

Terry Wild photographs in a bleak world of highways, gas stations, automobiles and mobile homes. It is a world built by and for people, yet there are no people in it. In his pictures, empty roads hide the soil. Often the horizon is blocked by chunks of concrete or metal. Overhead, a rain-filled sky presses down.

There is a kind of desolate poetry in these images, a sense of loss and loneliness—and even resignation, since he presents no alternative to the oppressive rule of inanimate objects. At the same time the photographs possess a bare and austere beauty that verges on the abstract. The shapes are few and simple, and they are fitted together with masterful logic and precision. Patches of texture and detail relieve broad areas of contrasting darks and lights. Overall, the cool, deliberate composition of visual elements seems to be the work of a formalist artist even more than a poet.

In his own mind, however, Terry Wild is neither poet nor formalist; he conceives his role to be that of a social critic and a moralist, who by his photographs comments on the world around him. He is obsessed by what he perceives as the subordination of the natural landscape to the hollow and lifeless apparatus of transportation. He wants to see a world in which roads or vehicles serve men and fit harmoniously into the landscape. But his pictures record a world in which the concrete and metal have taken over and extinguished both man and nature. The result is paralysis, a peopleless world in which nothing is alive, nothing moves.

In many of these pictures, mobile homes appear as a symbol of a loss of human values in present-day America. Wild remembers first noticing mobile homes when he was a student at the Art Center College of Design in Los Angeles. He was deeply disturbed by these particular artifacts of mobility. To him, they seemed the ultimate expression of rootlessness; because they could go anywhere, he sensed that they belonged nowhere. When he returned to his home in Williamsport, Pennsylvania, he found them proliferating there too. Most of these photographs were taken near his home in an effort to understand what was happening to his own life and the life of his community. Now 27 years old, he teaches part time at Lycoming College in Williamsport and works as a freelance photographer, exploring the look of a culture that he feels has sold its soul.

School Bus Stop

*Between a highway and a graveyard stands a
little white hut used by schoolchildren waiting
for their bus on cold winter days. It is late
afternoon, and heavy clouds are closing in. The
only hint of life is the shadow of the photographer
falling inconspicuously across the road.*

Gas Island

*A roadside filling station—its pumps and lights
and concrete base utterly alien to the landscape
of farmland and trees—sits in an empty field
like a spaceship from another planet.*

Used Automobiles

*Shot from a low angle, automobiles on a used-car
lot are rendered as threatening presences
that appear to exist in a state lying
somewhere between motion and nonmotion.*

Mobile Home Sales Lot No. 1

*Seen against a lowering sky, three mobile homes
on a sales lot appear as a phalanx of tyrannical
machine-age dinosaurs that have invaded the land
and blocked off any view of the horizon.*

Obstructed View

In a rural landscape, the hulk of an automobile angling in from one side seems a harbinger of asphalt and concrete to come, and a For Sale sign in the car's window adds a disturbing undertone to the sense of dislocation.

Mobile Home Sales Lot No. 2

*Machine coldly nuzzles machine at a sales lot for
mobile homes. In the absence of people, the sleek
design of the automobile and decorative touches
of the homes seem strangely meaningless.*

Mobile Home

*Set in a barren world of asphalt and electric wires,
a mobile home with a low gable and fake
clapboard siding stretches beyond both edges of
the picture—as though it goes on forever.*

133

Marcia Resnick: Pop-up People

There is a cheerful and yet slightly wacky feeling about the semisuburban world that Marcia Resnick photographs. The grownups or children pose at relaxed attention against a background of shaded lawns, small houses and quiet streets—subject matter typical of snapshots from a family photograph album. But the background is shown in the grays of the monochrome photograph, while the people are usually brightly colored and stand out against their surroundings like pop-up dolls.

This cardboard cutout look is achieved by the simplest means: Resnick leaves the background of the pictures untouched, but she paints over the people in toyshop hues, reducing the varied darks and lights of the photographic image to a few flat, hard-edged tones of a by-the-numbers coloring book. Yet the effect she achieves by this rudimentary device is subtle and complex. Suddenly the people and their world no longer seem to belong to one another. And, most peculiar and disconcerting of all, they do not appear to realize that anything is awry.

Resnick regards these pictures as explorations of various sorts of psychic space—a space that lies between people and their environment ("The two are alienated," she says), and a space that exists by virtue of the viewer's different levels of interest ("When you look at a snapshot, you are usually more interested in the people than the environment."). These vital hiatuses are instantly defined by the distinction between painted and nonpainted elements in the picture, and they are further defined by exaggerations of the two visual modes: the painting is simplified to the point of crudity, and the black-and-white portions are printed in such a way that they have a "gritty, dime-store look." Sometimes Resnick puts a new twist on these techniques, applying monochrome paints that match the tones of the black-and-white photographs. In one series of sequential images of a man driving along in a car *(pages 136-138),* she chose this method to emphasize the changing of light from moment to moment. Her intent was to point up the existence of still another kind of space—an Einsteinian space that is inextricably bound up with time.

Resnick, now 23, studied at The Cooper Union in New York City, has taught at the California Institute of the Arts and is currently teaching photography at Queens College in New York.

Mom and Dad

Says Resnick: "This is a picture of mom and dad and their house and their bushes and their lawn in Brooklyn." True enough—but a coloring-book treatment transforms this familiar world of her childhood into a two-layered reality.

William Hobart Thrall Driving

In three sequential images, the play of light on a driver's hands and arms is sharpened and simplified by the application of black, white and gray oil paints. The result is a mind-teasing mosaic of painting and photography—and a dazzling evocation of passing time.

The Hockey Player

This is a boy dressed for a roller-skate hockey game on a Brooklyn street. But he has been transformed by Marcia Resnick's playful paintbrush into a slightly cockeyed creature stranded on a planet remote from his own.

Colorado Lady

Although taken at a Colorado rodeo, this picture could have been made at any suburban cookout anywhere. The orange-haired lady and a woman in the background whose dress has been painted seem perfectly at home, unaware of how strange their world is.

The Marketplace

Important evolutionary shifts were underway in the photographic marketplace in 1973. While the pool of trained photographers seemed to be growing at an unprecedented rate, some of the most visible markets for photographers' work appeared to be fading away. This paradox is explored in a broad survey of opportunities in the field. It leads to surprising conclusions about photographic education and turns up little-known facts about the ways professionals earn a living. Among them are markets that barely existed a few years ago, such as photo safaris. Safaris burgeoned in 1973. For some professionals, they provided job opportunities; for amateurs they offered picture taking, leading to such rewards as the striking photographs displayed on pages 158-166.

Art serves commerce in a picture of a fork taken ▶ for a silverware manufacturer's advertising campaign. Horowitz' elegant photograph, with its imaginative use of a model's silhouetted face to dramatize the pattern of the silver, is an example of the high-quality work required for success in today's highly competitive photographic markets.

RYSZARD HOROWITZ: *Silver Fork*

Photography Boom or Bust?

In March 1973 the 10th annual conference of the Society for Photographic Education drew 164 participants from all over America to the University of New Mexico. The very existence of the society underscored the boom in photographic education that has taken place in the last decade. Yet only three months before the March meeting of the educators was held, LIFE, the last of the U.S. general-interest magazines—and thus the last mass-circulation showcase for photography—had suspended publication for the time. The near coincidence of these two events struck a great many observers as a sign of the dislocation between training and the jobs available for the trainees. Was the boom in photographic education leading to a bust in the photographic market?

Certainly the growth of education has been proceeding at a dizzying pace. Before the Second World War, photography was seldom taught on the university level, and college students who wanted to learn it did so on their own. By 1964, however, it was reported that more than 30 American universities and colleges were offering various degrees in photography, and within seven years the number of such institutions had increased to a total of more than 300, according to surveys made by Dr. C. William Horrell, a member of the Department of Cinema and Photography at Southern Illinois University. Nearly 50,000 college students in the United States and Canada were reported enrolled in photographic courses in Horrell's 1971 survey—almost twice the number enrolled only three years before.

Simultaneously with the rise in the number of college level photography students, however, two great social changes of the postwar period—the advent of television as the primary visual communications medium and the growth of the suburbs—combined to knock out a number of important markets for photographers, most of them in photojournalism. In the 20 years between 1953 and 1973 the number of major newspapers in the 10 largest cities in the United States declined from 43 to 26. In the same two decades, every mass-circulation, picture-oriented magazine produced in the United States ceased publication, permanently or temporarily. *Collier's* collapsed in 1956, *The Saturday Evening Post* in 1969 and *Look* in 1971. LIFE was suspended late in 1972.

LIFE and *Look* in particular had been prized markets for the best in magazine photography, and when those markets disappeared, shock waves of disbelief and despair were widely felt among professional photographers. To some it seemed that photojournalism had died with the suspension of LIFE. Others were less pessimistic, but even the optimists believed that photography had reached the end of an era, and wondered what the upcoming photographers would do. Would the profession be inundated with an oversupply of graduates from the burgeoning photography courses in the

TED WATHEN: *Building a Better Way to See the U.S.A.*

An implacable kudzu vine descends like a curtain before a shiny new car in this picture, made by one of the more than 100 photography students at the University of Florida. The partially reversed tones of the print, produced by "solarizing" it with a flash of light during development, make the picture an eerie counter-advertisement for a heavily mechanized society.

The eyes of two Halloween party revelers—one painted black, the other white—glare supernaturally in the light from photographer Luther Smith Jr.'s flash unit. Smith, who is a graduate student at Rhode Island School of Design, used infrared film in his camera and a dark red filter on his flash to subdue its light.

Arno Rafael Minkkinen, one of 28 graduate students in the Department of Photography, made this unusual self-portrait while studying at Rhode Island School of Design. He put his camera down on the boardwalk at Narragansett Beach and set the self-timer on the shutter release. Then lying down on the steps leading to the boardwalk in front of the camera, he rolled his head back, opened his mouth and let the camera record him as a tortured creature on an alien shore.

LUTHER SMITH JR.: *R.I.S.D.*

ARNO RAFAEL MINKKINEN: *Narragansett, Rhode Island*

ARNOLD NEWMAN: *Marcel Duchamp*

universities? Or are there perhaps unexplored aspects of the seemingly bleak situation that could transform it into something less grim than it appears on the surface?

These questions are hard to answer, given the complex mixture of customs, technology, economics and art that is photography. For one thing, there are no hard statistics on the marketplace. But a close look at photography in 1973 suggests that some people overreacted to the disasters striking the big picture magazines.

The achievements of LIFE and *Look* were real and great, and the photographers who worked for them were superstars whose well-publicized achievements brought much deserved glory to their profession. However, even in their heyday, LIFE and *Look* gave regular employment to just a handful of top photographers. So when those magazines suspended publication, only a few photographers were actually put out of work and all of them soon found employment in other areas of photography.

The big picture magazines, in spite of their visibility, were merely the tip of the iceberg of photojournalism, and photojournalism itself is only one of a great many icebergs in the big sea of professional photography. Among the myriad ways in which professionals earn a living, from covering weddings to recording the violent collisions between subatomic particles, advertising photography is still the most lucrative field of them all. Annual reports to corporations' stockholders are offering new opportunities. Filmstrips and other audio-visual projects form a growing market for photographers whose interests lead them in that direction. Industrial photography continues to provide remunerative if unpublicized work. Even photojournalism, though not in the best of health, is still alive.

The oldest branch of professional photography—and the one that has the largest number of practitioners—is portraiture. According to figures published by the Bureau of the Census in 1971, there are approximately 20,000 "portrait and commercial" photography studios in the United States. Opportunities in this field vary widely, but a man who is in business for himself in a small suburban community can earn from $5,500 to $25,000 a year, while a photographer working for one of the big studios might earn $20,000.

If portraiture is the meat and potatoes of professional photography, fashion is its caviar. But even this field—once one of the most innovative—has lost some zest. "It seems glamorous but it's always been hard work," says one leading practitioner, Hiro. "I don't photograph the fashion. I photograph the girl. The attitude has changed." Editorial policy of fashion magazines has become more conservative than it used to be, he points out. Where once Hiro created trends with his pictures, now he simply reports.

Hiro also does advertising—"That's where my income is," he says. This

◄ An elaborately carved chair in artist Marcel Duchamp's apartment complements his craggy features in a portrait by Arnold Newman, one of a handful of famous portraitists among the thousands of photographers in the field. For this picture, Newman used reflected light from a single flood lamp to make Duchamp's face stand out dramatically against the dark chair.

HIRO: *Model in Feathers*

Years of work as a fashion photographer have sharpened Hiro's instinct for coaxing nuances of expression from his model. The sidelong glance of this woman gives her a sophisticated air exactly suited to her elegant costume—which is the real subject of the picture.

field has been the richest market for professional photographers from the time of Edward Steichen *(pages 211-221),* and today it continues to provide a good living for a large number of seasoned specialists. Contenders for advertising assignments include everybody from experienced photojournalists like Ernst Haas and Alfred Eisenstaedt to beginning photographers just out of school, and prices vary widely according to the assignment and the photographer. A newcomer breaking into the field might get as little as $150 for a black-and-white advertisement in a small-circulation trade magazine devoted to news of a particular industry or profession. At the other end of the scale a top photographer can be paid upward of $4,000 for a two-page color advertisement that will appear in a number of large-circulation magazines. If he is willing to brave the uncertainties of a fluctuating market, a medium successful advertising photographer can net from $15,000 to $30,000 a year. Highly respected professionals like Hiro can earn considerably more.

Such pay is considered high by the standards of other branches of photography, but most of them offer reasonably good remuneration. Photography for annual reports is a field that has become prominent only in recent years, as more and more large corporations try to dress up the financial reports they are legally required to issue to their thousands of stockholders. Each year hundreds of corporations employ professional photographers to illustrate their annual reports. A few firms that take special pride in the appearance of their reports spend upward of $100,000 on them in a good year. A photography assignment for an annual report can range from a few stock shots of executives and plants to a full-dress photo essay in the best traditions of the big picture magazines.

This field is highly competitive, and at its best the work is hard but interesting and rewarding. "You're completely on your own, acting as art director and designer as well as photographer," says Wolf von dem Bussche, who has done dozens of annual reports for various corporations in the past four years. "You have to have a quick eye and be well-organized and experienced." Annual-report photographers frequently have to crisscross the country in order to cover a corporation's widespread operations, and they cannot afford to retrace their steps to correct omissions or errors. The work tends to be seasonal, usually from October to March, since annual reports are mailed to stockholders between the end of the company's fiscal year —often December 31—and the stockholders' annual meeting, usually held in the spring. When the economy is weak or when business is bad, companies frequently cut back on this kind of spending, but in good times annual reports pay very well. The average photographer earns around $500 a day on these assignments, and the best can earn $50,000 or more during the six-month "season."

WOLF von dem BUSSCHE: *Seals*

150

*Pictures of products as unfamiliar as these seals,
made by the Esterline Corporation for nuclear
reactors, increase an annual report's interest.
Many companies call on well-known freelances
like Wolf von dem Bussche for such photographs.*

WOLF von dem BUSSCHE: *Ionization Gauge Tubes*

Another photograph taken by the same photographer for an Esterline Corporation annual report shows a different kind of product —a sensitive instrument used in laboratories to measure extreme vacuums.

Photography for audio-visual presentations—slides and filmstrips accompanied by sound recordings—is another growing field for professionals. It stretches all the way from lavish promotions for airlines and motion-picture companies to instructional programs for teachers to use in schoolrooms. Photographers are usually employed when the producers cannot use existing photographs or need to have pictures that conform exactly to a shooting script. The photographer's job often entails searching out the most appropriate locations, hiring and costuming suitable models and finding authentic props. Sometimes the work is done by staff photographers who work full time for audio-visual companies, but a number of small companies prefer to use freelance photographers. Freelances are usually paid a minimum suggested by a professional association, the American Society of Magazine Photographers (ASMP); the current rate is $200 a day.

The audio-visual field includes some of the most challenging creative work found in photography today. One example is the series, "Profiles of Black Achievement," produced for schoolroom use by Guidance Associates of Pleasantville, New York. "In 'Black Achievement' we wanted to let the people tell their own stories," says Ron Tunison, one of the staff photographers who worked on this series. "So we photographed them in the places where they work and also at different spots where events in their lives took place." Other projects that have recently been undertaken by various producers of audio-visual programs include filmstrips about the lives and works of famous writers, studies of political events, surveys of urban and environmental problems, and dramatic re-creations of noteworthy historical events.

Another unsung area of photography, but one that provides jobs for thousands of photographers, is industrial photography. Many companies do not require a full-time photography staff and hire freelances to do their work. Some freelances specialize in industrial work while others, who make their living primarily from advertising, may take only occasional industrial assignments. But upward of 16,000 U.S. companies have full-time photography departments. Bethlehem Steel, for example, has a staff of eight photographers and 16 photographic technicians who work at its corporate headquarters in Bethlehem, Pennsylvania. Most of Bethlehem Steel's industrial photographs are records of developments in the company's complex operations—not the sort of thing to set a photographer's creative juices to running. But industrial photography can also involve scientific studies and visual aids, which give photographers more scope for ingenuity and originality and occasionally the opportunity for such a dramatic picture as the shot of an oil rig on page 154, made for an oil-well-drilling contractor.

Finally, there is photojournalism, still an important field despite the recent troubles that have beset the big picture magazines. Arthur Rothstein, who was formerly the director of *Look*'s Photographic Department and who is now Associate Editor of *Parade,* feels that the absence of the big magazines has not really caused much change. "In New York things seem tough because there is a great concentration of photographers here. But there has been a kind of decentralization of photography since the old times at *Look* and LIFE, and outside of New York, especially, photojournalists do well." Rothstein points out that more than 100 new magazines began publication in 1972 and he believes the market they offer more than makes up for the loss of sales to *Look* and LIFE.

Many of the new magazines appearing on the stands are aimed at special-interest groups, from country-music fans to shopping-center operators. Usually their budgets are limited and they are seldom able to pay photographers more than the ASMP minimum of $200 a day—sometimes less. However, as small as they are, they represent additions to a number of older, more established publications that continue to survive in good health and still use journalistic photographs in substantial numbers. Among them are the Sunday newspaper magazines, the airlines' magazines, controlled-circulation magazines such as Diners Club's *Signature* and American Express' *Travel & Leisure,* regional magazines such as *New York, Atlanta* and *Boston,* flourishing national magazines such as *Ebony, National Geographic, Holiday* and *Rolling Stone,* and a number of popular picture magazines in Europe and in Latin America.

In addition to the healthy tribe of magazines there are the newspapers: big regional daily newspapers such as the Louisville *Courier-Journal, The Topeka Daily Capital,* the *Minneapolis Tribune, The Houston Post* and *The Denver Post* as well as the myriads of smaller daily and weekly papers. Several of the regional dailies have been redesigned and reorganized to make greater use of photographs. The increased use of offset printing in the production of newspapers, which sharply reduces the cost of reproducing photographs, enables many low-budget weeklies to carry more pictures than used to be possible.

In all these fields—as important to the future of professional photography as they are—there is not, to be sure, much of the glamour and excitement of the great days of LIFE and *Look*. Professional photography today is increasingly anonymous, and any young photographer who expects to achieve the renown of a David Douglas Duncan or a Margaret Bourke-White is inviting almost certain disappointment. Whether he also risks frustration in an attempt to earn an ordinary living depends on how stiff the competition is for the existing jobs—and the magnitude of the competition, present and future, is not easily estimated. The statistics on photographic education afford only a useful hint or two.

These 20 pictures are only a sample of the hundreds of unusual slides that make up Harvey Lloyd's three-screen audio-visual extravaganza, "Family of Earth." In producing the show for the United Nations Conference on the Human Environment, Lloyd traveled 50,000 miles, served as writer, photographer, director and even put together the production's musical sound track.

JAY MAISEL: *Neptune 7*

Freelance Jay Maisel's photograph of Neptune 7, an offshore drilling rig that petroleum companies lease to explore for oil, was made originally for the rig's designer and owner, Schlumberger Limited. This shot is only one of a take including several pictures that have been widely used: on the cover of an annual report, in an advertising campaign and even in technical articles.

For while there may be an astonishing number of college-level photography courses, and an equally astounding number of young people enrolled in them, it is clear that not all photography students plan to make a career in the field. Horrell's 1971 survey found that of the 50,000 photography students in American colleges and universities, only about 1,500—fewer than 3 per cent—were graduating with majors in photography. The rest were subordinating photography to other majors or merely taking a course or two as part of a liberal-arts education.

Horrell's series of surveys also confirmed a suspicion, widely held, that much of photographic education was not intended to be useful job preparation. The clue lies in the changing role of photography courses within the universities. Horrell established that the recent growth in photographic courses has taken place more in departments of fine arts than in departments of journalism, which have been the traditional academic parent of photography. In 1964 he reported that photography was taught in twice as many departments of journalism as departments of fine arts. By the time of his 1968 survey, however, the number of art departments offering photography courses had more than doubled, almost catching up to the number of journalism departments, which had increased only marginally during the same four years. In 1971 the number of art departments teaching photography nearly doubled again, while the number of journalism departments teaching photography actually declined. As a result, art departments have now taken over the lead in photography education that had previously been held by journalism departments.

The significance of this turnabout becomes apparent when the photographic courses in the two departments are compared with one another. In the departments of journalism, the emphasis is very much on the job to be done rather than on the artistic development of the photographer. "We're not putting out photographers in the manner of Minor White or the more non-literal or artistically inclined," says Harris Smith, who teaches photojournalism at Boston University. "Our students are encouraged to pursue a very practical course."

Most of the career-oriented photography studies tend to be highly specialized. Students concentrate their attention on particular fields such as architectural photography, advertising illustration or medical-biological photography. The Rochester Institute of Technology, which has the oldest and biggest degree-granting photography program in the nation, offers plainly practical courses to its students, in everything from photographic illustration to photographic science and instrumentation; the courses require rigorous study of the scientific and technical aspects of photography as well as creative studies. At the Art Center College of Design in Los Angeles, which specializes in teaching advertising photography, most of the instructors are successful working professionals who also teach days or evenings. "Sometimes commercial work is very creative and sometimes it isn't," says Edward Handler of the Art Center College. "But we think in terms of professional photography. Our graduates are going to be paid by clients to resolve their photographic problems."

An entirely different approach to photographic education is generally found in the departments of fine arts. The emphasis in many of these schools is on the artistic type of photography that usually appears framed on the walls of museums and galleries, rather than on the type that most often appears in the pages of newspapers and magazines. Here the instruction often is conceived of not as vocational training but as part of a curriculum designed to enhance the student's awareness of himself and his world in the best liberal-arts tradition. "I'm not concerned with making photographers," says Jerry Uelsmann, Professor of Art at the University of Florida. "I'm concerned with making better people." Robert Heinecken, Associate Professor of Art at the University of California at Los Angeles, agrees. "The instruction is not geared to complete understanding in a vocational sense or professional or commercial sense. It is more oriented to their own needs, oriented more to their own interests."

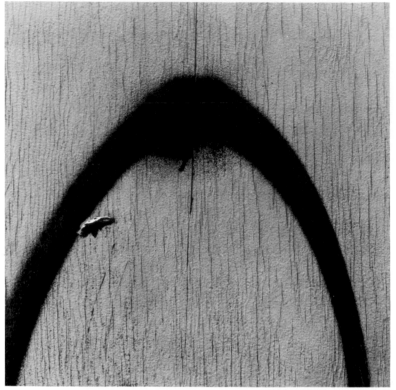

AARON SISKIND: *Providence 49*

The graduates of fine-arts departments who do prepare for careers in photography almost invariably want to teach rather than earn a living in a field such as advertising. Like their own teachers, they have learned that this is the best way to get on with their own photography. As university teaching jobs become filled up, some of these academic specialists are turning to high-school photography courses, while others are teaching adult education courses. Still others are becoming curators or curatorial assistants on the staffs of museums, many of which—after more or less neglecting photography—are now building extensive collections of photographic art.

These patterns in education indicate that the proliferating photography courses are concentrating on art rather than commerce, and thus the press of photography students on the job market, though serious, is not as serious as the growth in education might suggest. Much of the expansion is taking place in the fine-arts departments, where few students expect to make a living except as teachers, and even there most of the new photography students are not devoting their major efforts to photography. In the aftermath of the suspension of *Look* and LIFE, 50,000 students of photography seems an enormous number. But for most of them photography will be a source of delight and instruction, not a full-time job from which they must earn a living. For the rest, the road will be rough and crowded, and not everybody will make it to the end.

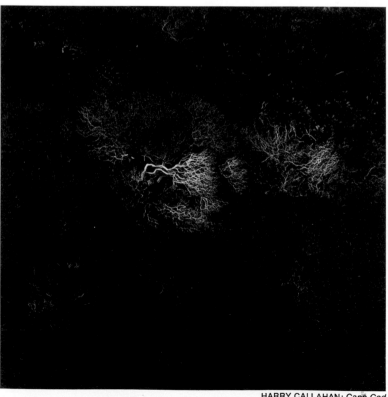

HARRY CALLAHAN: *Cape Cod*

The personal approach to photography taught in many university fine-arts courses is illustrated in pictures taken by Aaron Siskind and Harry Callahan, teachers at Rhode Island School of Design, and Jerry Uelsmann, who teaches at the University of Florida. Siskind, who photographed a fragment of graffiti sprayed onto an old wooden fence (top left), Callahan, who captured a silvery filigree of bare branches on Cape Cod (bottom left), and Uelsmann, who created an ominous composite photograph (right), all teach photography more as a means of self-expression than as a way to earn a living.

JERRY N. UELSMANN: *Herman*

157

Camera Safaris

The Arctic voyagers seen on these pages could easily be mistaken for a scientific expedition bent on establishing an outpost at the top of the world. Why else would a group of men and women venture into such a barren, inhospitable region? But they were not scientists. Like legions of amateur photographers in 1973, they were on a photo safari, demonstrating that a good picture is worth a thousand miles—or many thousands, for that matter. Such picture-taking tours, sponsored by travel agencies and airlines, carried price tags ranging from several hundred to several thousand dollars per person, and the size of the groups varied from less than 10 people to almost 2,000. But the real measure of the diversity—and thriving state—of photo safaris is suggested by their itineraries. The tours went about everywhere in the world—to Baja California for shots of gray whales mating in coastal lagoons, to the Yucatán for photographs of Maya ruins, to the remote wildlife paradise of the Galápagos Islands 650 miles off the coast of Ecuador (where Charles Darwin gleaned much of his evidence for the theory of evolution), to the pyramids along the Nile and the storied game preserves of East Africa and the steppes of Mongolia. The biggest and most unusual was not strictly photographic although its purpose was to take pictures—some 5,000 amateur and professional astronomers, most with camera-equipped telescopes, traveled by plane and boat to Africa to record the June 30 eclipse *(page 235)*. In one index to worldwide tours, the listing "Special Interests: Photography" is followed by nine pages of fine print.

The photo safari that went to the Arctic in 1973—the first one ever to breech that frontier—proved that any corner of the world, no matter how far away or inclement, is a feasible hunting ground for amateur photographers. This particular group of photographers, all Americans, boarded a Scandinavian ship and cruised for two weeks among Norway's Spitzbergen Islands, just above the Arctic Circle. Here they found photographic conditions permitting unusually effective pictures. The light is unique. With the sun at a low angle to the horizon for long periods of time, the effect is one of protracted twilight—a lighting condition preferred by many professionals for its contribution to mood and detail. In addition, the isolated mountain peaks and stretches of ice generate contrasts that provide dramatic views.

Taking advantage of these opportunities in a difficult environment proved to be an adventure accompanied by an appropriate share of adversities. The northern seas regularly rose in 30-foot waves, sending sheets of freezing spray over the decks, tossing passengers from their bunks and making most of them seasick. Quarters on the ship were appropriately rugged: there was one shower and toilet for the 18 passengers and crew. And the temperature seldom inched above 15°, even though the sun never set. Said one of the participants, Luis Villota, who took the pictures shown here and on

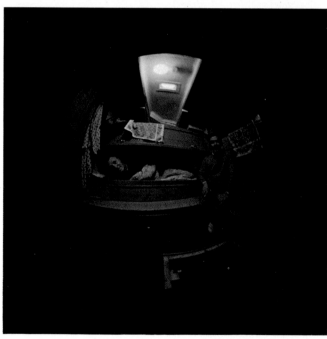

A fisheye lens gave this aerial view of the Signal Horn and the surrounding pack ice from the photo-safari ship's lookout mast (top). Belowdecks, the same lens generated a false sense of spaciousness in a picture of the photographer and a fellow passenger in their cramped six-by-eight-foot cabin.

On a rare sunny day, Luis Villota set his camera for delayed exposure and posed himself (top, far right) with his shipmates. The next day, when the ship reached the northernmost point of its voyage at latitude 81°, he used a 20mm wide-angle lens to show his fellow safari members gingerly exploring a large chunk of the pack ice.

the following pages, "It was an ordeal. But if you're afraid of hardship, you'd better stay home and look at someone else's pictures."

Photo safaris are a relatively recent phenomenon. While group tours have long bowed to the desire of travelers to take souvenir pictures during the trip, one enterprising United States travel agency in 1954 hit upon the idea of promoting a South American tour primarily as a photographic expedition to a remote region. The response was so positive that other agencies soon leaped into the field, designing trips specifically for photographers. Today, the promotional literature for such safaris often includes tips on the kind of equipment to take along; the advice almost always recommends a long-focal-length lens, warns against relying on new and untested gear (which would be difficult to replace or repair in remote areas), and advocates bringing a large supply of film ("as much as you think you will need . . . and then some," says one brochure). Since good photographs demand time and attention, tours are generally set at a leisurely pace. And many photo safaris are led by guides who are photographers in their own right; they know where the best locations are and they may even conduct seminars to help the traveler get the best possible pictures.

In Africa, some white hunters have traded in their elephant guns for cameras and have become photo-safari guides. "I'm all for camera safaris," says one former hunter. "People shoot straighter with a camera than with a gun." But other tours have enlisted the aid of some of the world's outstanding photographers to help amateurs bring back good pictures. In May 1973, LIFE photojournalist Alfred Eisenstaedt guided 30 camera-toting pilgrims through Brazil, taking them from the glitter of Rio de Janeiro to the dank mysteries of a mountain rain forest. The weight of Eisenstaedt's reputation had a curious effect on one of the members of the tour. Whenever Eisenstaedt finished shooting a picture, the faithful follower would quickly fill his vacated footprints, aim where he had aimed, and snap the picture—presumably with excellent results. But others on this and many different tours used their own eyes and brains. As Luis Villota said of his journey into the Arctic, the safari offered "extraordinary scenery unlike anything we'd ever seen before or will see again." He and his fellows made the most of it.

*Sheer cliffs and an eroded needle of rock are
sandwiched between fog and sea at Bear Island,
a possession of Norway and one of the most
isolated specks of land in the Arctic Ocean.*

Tailoring the choice of lenses for his 35mm SLR
to the demands of the scenery of Spitsbergen, at
a Norwegian island inside the Arctic Circle,
Villota used an unusually long focal length
—500mm—to reach out for a mountain adazzle in
a shaft of light (top left). A 50mm lens shows the
looming flanks of Hornsund Fjord (top right).
Another long lens—200mm—brings out the
elephant-hide texture of the Agardfi coast (bottom
left). And a wide-angle 20mm lens encompasses
the sweep of the Red River (bottom right).

A huge rain puddle mirrors an abandoned coal station at New Alesund, an important Norwegian mining community on Spitsbergen until the coal deposits gave out in the mid-1960s.

Water lines insulated against Arctic cold lead to a satellite-communications station at New Alesund, now a research center. Winter is so frigid scientists evacuate the station then.

The gleaming ramparts of a glacier rise within a Spitsbergen fjord. The crew chipped ice from one glacier and melted it for drinking water, which Villota remembers as "delicious."

In a landscape that seems almost as lifeless as the moon, a stream cuts through rock rubble and snowdrifts, which still bear ripple marks imprinted on them by the Arctic's fierce winter gales.

Melding the hues of summer and winter, Villota shot across the moss-covered green shore of King's Fjord in Spitsbergen to the icy blue-white range of mountains on the far side.

Poking its pinnacle through a low-hanging cloud,
one of Spitsbergen's Three Crown mountains
is a vision of glittering grandeur beyond the dark
mass of a peninsula in King's Fjord.

The Annual Awards

Ever since the Greeks bestowed laurel wreaths on athletes, poets and musicians, human societies have been conferring awards on those among their number who best expressed their ideals and most notably enriched their culture. Today, photographers come in for a richly deserved share of honors. They are given prizes for special contests that spotlight particular concerns of the culture; and they are given other prizes for answering these concerns during the everyday practice of their profession. The awards in 1973 fall into both categories, and some of the most widely coveted are shown on the following pages.

It is worthy of note that this year's award-winning pictures show far fewer scenes of violence than those of the past several years. Whether this bespeaks a worldwide sigh of relief at the winding down of the war in Vietnam or a general weariness with strife of all kinds is anyone's guess. But it seems certain that the temper of the times helps shape the taste of the photographers who take the pictures and of the judges who rate them. Both sets of award-winning photographs shown here thus reflect the aspirations—as well as the action—of life as it was lived in 1973.

WILLIAM BORNEFELD

In this picture from the photographic essay that won the Grand Prize in the LIFE bicentennial photography contest, Mrs. Blanche Murphy faces the world alone, as her relatives conclude a visit after the death of her 96-year-old mother.

The LIFE Contest

What was perhaps the most ambitious photographic contest ever held, initiated by LIFE magazine, attracted entries from some 15,000 photographers competing for a total of $47,000 in prize money—of which an unprecedented $25,000 was set aside for a single grand prize. The theme honored the approaching bicentennial anniversary of the beginning of the American Revolution and called for pictures relating to "A Declaration of Interdependence." Beyond this broad requirement, few rules limited the entrants; they could be either amateur or professional, and were simply asked to submit portfolios of their work, including at least three but not more than 12 pictures, which demonstrated the dependence of Americans on one another and on their environment. Since at the time the entries were judged LIFE magazine was not being published, the winners are being presented in the 1974 edition of PHOTOGRAPHY YEAR.

Choosing the winners proved a formidable task, for during the two years that the contest was underway, a total of 150,000 pictures was submitted. In September 1973 a panel of seven judges closeted themselves for three days to examine the entries. By a combination of open discussion at first and a secret ballot at the conclusion of their deliberations, they reached the decisions on the photographs shown here. The Grand Prize went to a series that formed a classic photojournalistic essay; it depicts a phase in the lives of an elderly mother and daughter *(right)*. Eight other prizes, ranging from $5,000 to $1,000, went to four professionals and four amateurs for pictures showing modern Americans dealing with their lives in varying degrees of simplicity and complexity *(pages 172-177)*.

It is a significant index of the times that most of the contestants interpreted the theme of interdependence as pertaining to ecology, and most of the photographs therefore depicted scenes from nature. But the judges interpreted the theme more broadly, and all the pictures that were given awards explore qualities of human life. Aside from their thematic content, the photographs were judged less on technical virtuosity than on artistic sensitivity and the photographers' ability to express something of themselves in the pictures they took. Many of the contestants sent letters with their entries; but, as one judge said, "The best pictures stood on their own." Another added: "I am most impressed when I can sense the personality of the photographer coming through in his pictures. I feel that the photographers should be involved with their material and have the courage to take pictures of what is going on in their lives and in the lives around them."

All the pictures shown here do reflect such an involvement, whether their subjects do nothing more remarkable than casually face a summer's morning from their own front door *(page 175)* or whether, as in the photographs that won the Grand Prize, the confrontation is with death.

William Bornefeld—Grand Prize ($25,000)
Mrs. Cora Graham, 96, rocks in a chair while her daughter, Mrs. Blanche Murphy, 72, dozes on a couch beside her, in one of a series of photographs documenting the relationship between the two old women. They lived together in a 100-year-old house with a wood stove for heat, water brought to the kitchen in jugs, and only each other for company.

At left, Mrs. Murphy frets over her mother, who is about to be hospitalized after a stroke and will no longer be in her daughter's care. A month later, Mrs. Graham died, and friends and relatives gathered at the funeral to pay their respects. Below, Mrs. Murphy's sister wipes away tears of grief.

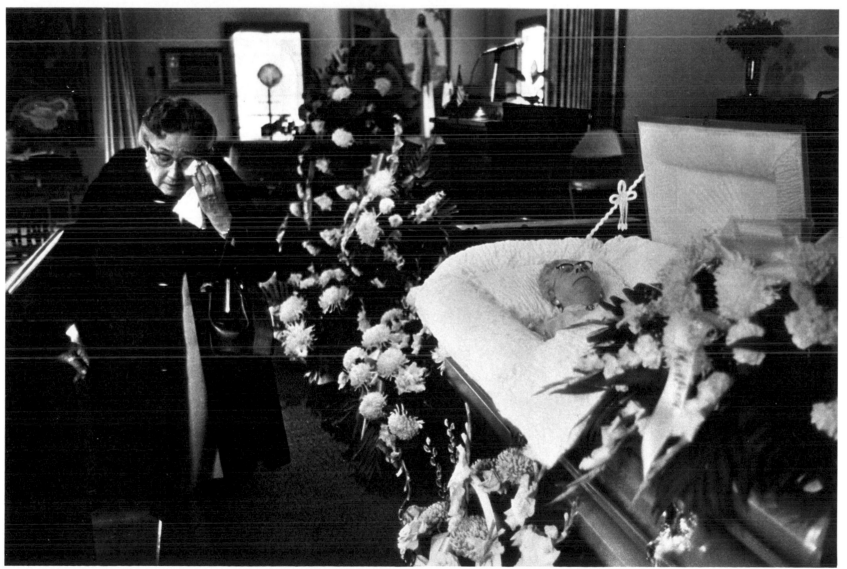

Martin Benjamin—1st Prize Professional ($5,000)

The generation gap appears in these two pictures. Three boys in Albany, New York (top) find their own amusement while an old woman stares in concentration. At bottom, spectators at a rock concert hear the same music but the older face appears set against it, the younger one receptive.

James Barker—2nd Prize Professional ($3,000)

Bedtime romps unite some of the nine children of the Lew Gardner family in Oakland, California, whose life together is the subject of this prize project. Here three-and-a-half-year-old Lizzie belly-flops into bed as her younger brother Tim stands in the corner waiting his turn.

Bill Owens—3rd Prize Professional ($2,000)

The same photographs for which photographer Owens won the LIFE contest third prize for professionals have since been published in a book entitled "Suburbia." His prizewinning photographs are not shown in this space because they appear in the section on books (page 50).

Simon Cherpitel—4th Prize Professional ($1,000)

A black man and a white woman, photographed at their wedding in California, portray a trust in each other that transcends the suspicion and hostility often manifest between members of their races. Cherpitel, who runs a gallery, took this portrait as a wedding present for the couple.

Cliff Feulner—1st Prize Amateur ($5,000)

Alone among the prizewinners, photographer Cliff Feulner answered the contest's theme of interacting relationships by inventing his own scene—creating a composite photograph with the help of scissors and paste. For this picture, he cut the figures out of different photographs, pasted them to white cardboard, painted a piece of construction equipment in the lower right corner, and spread some dirt and sand on the card to represent the ground. Feulner then made a color slide of this collage and combined it with a slide of the sky to finish the picture—a vivid scene of children absorbed in grownups' work.

Richard Albertine
—2nd Prize Amateur ($3,000)

*On a Christmas night, the town square of
Marstons Mills—Richard Albertine's home on
Cape Cod—is an empty environment waiting for
people to bring it to life. A blurred image of
the photographer's dog, which ran into the
picture during the long exposure, seems a
ghostly reminder of the town's busier hours.*

*Jean Albertine, the photographer's wife,
happened to come to the door in topless undress
with their son Kelly one summer's morning
while her husband was experimenting in the yard
with an antique camera he had just bought.
She lingered to watch, providing the photographer
with a spontaneous and intimate portrait
of his family framed in their own doorway.*

Clara Bulkley—3rd Prize Amateur ($2,000)

Sampling the spectrum of moods that occur in a family's life together, the photographer caught her sister and brothers in attitudes of serenity, aloofness, mirth and nonchalance.

Gregory Pile—4th Prize Amateur ($1,000)

A hesitant trust seems to emanate from this wordless boy, a patient in a California hospital for the mentally retarded. The portrait is part of a photographic story on the hospital's inmates.

Worldwide Prizes

For every photograph that is specifically intended for submission to a contest, there are hundreds taken by professional photographers as part of their job. Winning prizes may have been the furthest thing from a photographer's mind when he created a great picture in the line of work. Happily, the field of photography abounds in awards that can be conferred without being sought. Some such awards come from esthetic and honorary societies, such as those that annually grant the Prix Niepce in France *(opposite)* and the Nendo Sho in Japan *(pages 182-183);* they exist for the purpose of fostering photography as one of the arts. Other citations come from the makers of photographic equipment, whose aim is to combine commercial self-interest with the advancement of photographic expertise and the raising of esthetic standards. But far and away the most conspicuous use of photography is in journalism; hence most photographic awards originate with journalistic societies and are won by journalistic photographers.

In recent times—since World War II at least—the dominant themes of award-winning photographs have, more often than not, been violence, death and destruction. Perhaps the spectacle of violence wins a fascinated audience in any era; a photograph can represent it in a form that is both explicit and emotion-charged without threatening the viewer. In any case, the prevalence of such photographs is an accurate measure of the era we live in. Violence has become an inescapable part of international and domestic life, and journalistic photographers have perforce recorded it.

This year, however, pictures of horrifying, gruesome or catastrophic events are in the minority. Only two of the year's major award-winning photographs confront the tragedies of war head on *(pages 185 and 186).* Instead, peace, serenity and durability were discerned in a multitude of guises. One photographer even found a scene of pastoral calm right in the middle of war-torn North Vietnam *(page 182).* In Japan a photographer discovered a ready audience for nostalgia *(page 183),* and another capitalized on the universal human capacity for fantasy *(page 183).* And one brand new award—conferred by a school of journalism and co-sponsored by a camera company—underscores the search for tranquillity: the World Understanding Award honors a "conscious effort to promote world understanding through photography." The first winner of this award portrayed a tribe of Philippine aborigines *(page 181)*—a people who never strike their children, who seldom kill anything larger than fish for food, and who have no word for war.

Le Prix Niepce—France

Inventive technique characterizes the work of ▶ Albert Visage, who won the Prix Niepce, given each year to a promising young French photographer. He photographed this troupe of touring Cossack performers as they rehearsed their colorful act in a meadow. By lying on the ground and using a 200mm lens, Visage isolated the horsemen against the sky; and by using a slow shutter speed, he created just enough blur to suggest motion and excitement.

ALBERT VISAGE: *Cossacks*, 1972

Magazine Photographer of the Year

This picture, showing a fireman pulling a car's flaming innards onto the street where they can be extinguished, was part of a group for which Co Rentmeester was honored. It illustrated an article about the busiest firehouse in the world, one of five stories that appeared in LIFE in 1972, and won Rentmeester election as Magazine Photographer of the Year by the University of Missouri School of Journalism and the National Press Photographers Association—which also awarded the prizes on the opposite page.

CO RENTMEESTER: *Bronx Fire*, 1972

JOHN LAUNOIS: *Lubu,* 1972

Nikon World Understanding Award—U.S.A.

*Lubu, a member of the newly discovered Tasaday
tribe, plays in the Philippine jungle. For such
photographs, which gave the world its first view of
the gentle, stone-age Tasaday, John Launois
received the Nikon World Understanding Award.*

KURT E. SMITH: *Teenage Idol,* 1972

Newspaper Photographer of the Year—U.S.A.

*Kurt Smith, whose visual insight won him the
Newspaper Photographer of the Year award,
captured in this picture of a country-music star and
his wife two sides of rural folk—their stolid
quality and their rambunctious way of having fun.*

181

BUNYO ISHIKAWA: *Mud for the Dikes*, 1972

Nendo Sho (Annual Award)—Japan

*It does not matter that war rages about them;
North Vietnamese farmers must haul mud to repair
the dikes along the Red River just as they
have for centuries. This mistily peaceful picture
helped earn the Japan Photography Society
award for photojournalist Bunyo Ishikawa.*

Nendo Sho (Annual Award)—Japan

Does she harvest henbane and belladonna or daisies and petunias? Is she a witch or a nymph, mad or sane? For the haunting ambiguity of this and other photographs in a book entitled "Nadia: The Dollhouse in the Forest," Hajime Sawatari was voted an annual award from the Japan Photography Society.

Nendo Sho (Annual Award)—Japan

On a sunny day in 1940, Koji Morooka photographed spectators watching sailors of the Imperial Japanese Navy line up for a parade on the square in front of the Emperor's palace. The picture appeared in Morooka's book "Remembrance of Tokyo," a collection of views spanning more than four decades, which won an award from the Japan Photography Society.

HAJIME SAWATARI: *Forest Sprite*, 1971

KOJI MOROOKA: *Naval Memorial Day*, 1940

183

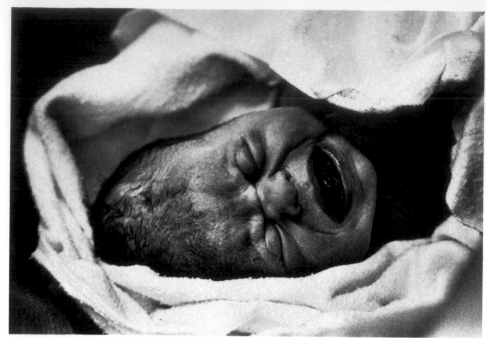

Pulitzer Prize for Feature Photography —U.S.A.

Faces tell the story of one family's experience with natural childbirth in these pictures by Brian Lanker, winner of the Pulitzer Prize for Feature Photography. The expressions of the newborn daughter and her father, both fresh from the delivery room, reflect entirely different impressions of their recent adventures.

BRIAN LANKER: *Jacki Lynn Coburn,* 1972

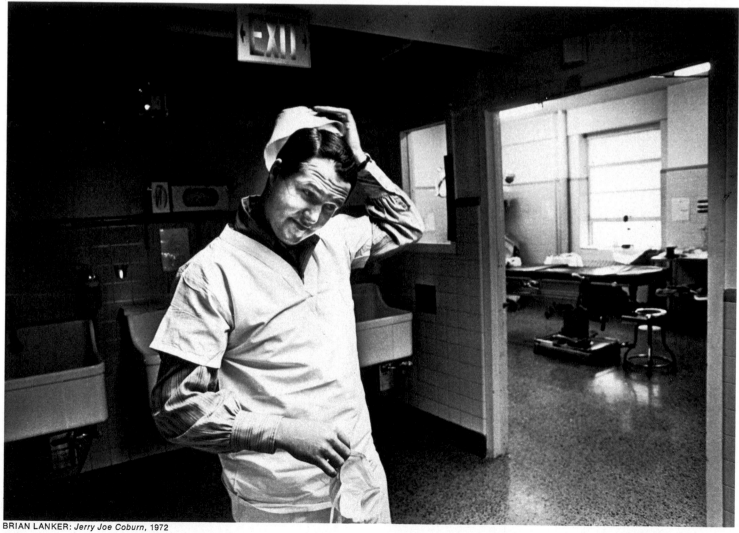

BRIAN LANKER: *Jerry Joe Coburn,* 1972

HUYNH CONG UT: *The Terror of War*, 1972

Pulitzer Prize for Spot News—U.S.A.
Press Photo of the Year Award—The Netherlands

*In a distillation of the pain of war that earned
dual awards for South Vietnamese photojournalist
Huynh Cong Ut, a terrified young victim of
misaimed napalm runs naked and screaming
down a road after shedding her flaming clothing.*

Robert Capa Gold Medal—U.S.A.

Threatening yet vulnerable in his outsized gas mask, an eight-year-old lad stands ready with a Molotov cocktail in a Catholic ghetto in Northern Ireland. Clive Limpkin, winner of the Robert Capa Gold Medal for news pictures of the strife between Catholics and Protestants, photographed the boy as he and his companions harassed police.

CLIVE LIMPKIN: *Boy in Northern Ireland, 1973*

186

The New Technology

The techniques for producing color prints and transparencies in the home darkroom have been so complicated that few amateur photographers spent the time and money to try them. Color film was generally sent off to commercial laboratories for processing. Those photographers who insisted on personal control over their pictures limited themselves, often reluctantly, to black-and-white pictures. In 1973, this situation showed signs of changing as new ways of processing color promised to get the job done simply, quickly and relatively inexpensively. How these new systems work and some examples of their visually stunning results are shown opposite and on pages 194-199.

There were also significant developments in cameras and lenses. Charts listing the specifications and cost of new models appear on pages 200-205, followed by reports on special news in technology.

A nude provides clear evidence of the quality of color reproduction possible with new simplified printmaking processes (pages 194-195). Flesh tones—for most viewers the crucial test of natural-looking color—appear realistic throughout.

EVA RUBINSTEIN: *Untitled*

Homemade Color Prints—Faster, Simpler

Little-heralded changes in color photography snowballed toward a full-scale revolution in 1973 with the announcement of two improved print systems. One made printing from color negative film almost as easy—and more important, as versatile—as black-and-white processing. The other brought to the small darkroom a previously unavailable color-slide-to-color-print technique that saves time and effort because it makes prints directly, dispensing with an intermediate negative, which had been required. While both these advances increased the importance of color work to photographers, it is the new ease of making prints from negatives that promises the greatest long-range influence on the course of the art.

For nearly 20 years the standard process used by commercial processors and individual photographers to make color prints from negatives has been Kodak's Ektacolor "C" system. But its use is not, like black-and-white processing, a simple matter of develop, fix and wash. It demands five separate chemical baths, four intermediate washes and upwards of half an hour per print. These complexities spurred both the giants of the photographic industry as well as some not-so-large innovators to find simpler ways for the photographer to produce quality color prints in his own darkroom, and a number of such negative printing systems have been introduced in recent years: Agfacolor, Colourtronic 32, FR Rapid Access, Kodak Ektaprint 3, Luminos, Spiratone B-85 and Unicolor B. All work with a variety of recently developed papers and require less time and fewer chemical baths than the earlier Ektacolor process, but the newest, the Color by Beseler color print process marketed in 1973, calls for only two baths, one wash and about seven minutes' time (for a step-by-step demonstration see pages 194-195). In fact, this process takes less time to make a color print than is normally needed for a black-and-white print.

Beseler accomplishes this simplification and time saving by eliminating and combining operations. The older methods required at least five separate steps: developing the image, stopping development, bleaching the image, fixing the image and finally stabilizing the image. In addition there were intermediate and final washes. Beseler dropped the intermediate washes and the stop bath. And because the bleaching and fixing compounds wash out easily, the stabilizer could be eliminated. Faster-acting chemicals reduce the time required to a minute in the developer at 107°, another minute at the same temperature in the combined bleach-fix and about five minutes of final washing at room temperature. The results can be superb, as the gallery of photographs by Fred Pleasure on pages 196-199 demonstrates. Beseler, as well as Colourtronic, FR, Spiratone and Unicolor, supplies plastic drums inside which the complete processing procedure is carried out after the room lights are turned on (the exposure of the print and

New Color Processes

Process	Paper Type Required	Package Sizes (Gallons of Working Solution)	Number of Steps		Time Required (Minutes)		Number of 8 x 10 Prints Per Gallon	Cost per 8 x 10 Print (Manufacturer's Estimate)
			Drum	Tray	Drum	Tray		
Agfacolor	B	1, 3½	7	6	9½	12½	32	55
Color by Beseler	A or B	¼, 1	3	3	7	7	100	55
Colourtronic 32	B	¼, ½, 1	7	6	10¾	9¾	64	49
Kodak Ektaprint 3	A	1, 3½	5	4	9	8	32	90
Luminos Color Chempak	B	½	6	5	7¾	7½	32	62
FR Rapid Access	B	½, 3	6	5	7¾	10	80	60
Spiratone B-85	B	½, 1, 2, 4, 10	6	5	7½	7½	64	40
Unicolor B	B	1, 4	6	5	9	7¾	60	63

Each of the eight new color printing processes described in the chart above must be used with paper—type A or type B—it is designed for. Even brands made for both types come in two formulations, one for each type of paper. All processes give good color, but vary in packaging, procedures and price.

the loading of it into the drum are, of course, done in total darkness).

The new slide-printing technique is not, strictly speaking, new, since it has been in use in large commercial laboratories since 1941. It eliminates the intermediate step of making a color negative by employing reversal printing paper, which gives an opaque color positive directly from positive transparency. But until 1973 the chemicals needed for processing this paper were not available in small quantities for home use.

Until now the number of photographers who have done their own color printing has been understandably small: the process has required too much time and fuss for most people. The greater speed and convenience of the new processes are changing this picture drastically. But they may have a more profound effect as well, increasing the value of color photography.

Many serious photographers have shied away from color entirely because they felt that they were unable to make prints for themselves and thus were denied full control over the final result. This limitation no longer exists. Color printmaking, once it moves out of a mass-production laboratory and into an individual laboratory, permits more manipulation than black-and-white printing. It opens a new world of creativity for photography. Artists who have long favored black-and-white prints as their medium may find that photographs in color have now become an equally challenging and rewarding form of expression.

Printing Slides Directly

The new ease in turning out color prints from color slides at home comes from the availability of reversal paper and chemicals, which eliminate the need for an intermediate negative. This paper, Kodak Ektachrome Type 1993, is made almost exactly like the film used for color slides except that the sensitized materials are mounted on opaque white paper instead of on clear plastic. Like most color films, it has three emulsion layers coupled with dyes that give a positive color image directly, as shown in the diagrams at right.

Some color balancing may be necessary, and filters can be employed to alter tones to correct errors or to create special effects. Exposure can also be varied from point to point in the image, just as in black-and-white enlarging, by blocking light from selected areas—dodging or burning-in. But remember that dodging and burning-in exchange their roles with reversal paper, since the more light that reaches the image the lighter it gets, not darker as in negative printing. Thus it is necessary to hold light back from overexposed areas and give more light to the underexposed ones. In addition, if white-bordered prints are desired, border areas must be exposed under the enlarger while the picture area is protected by a mask.

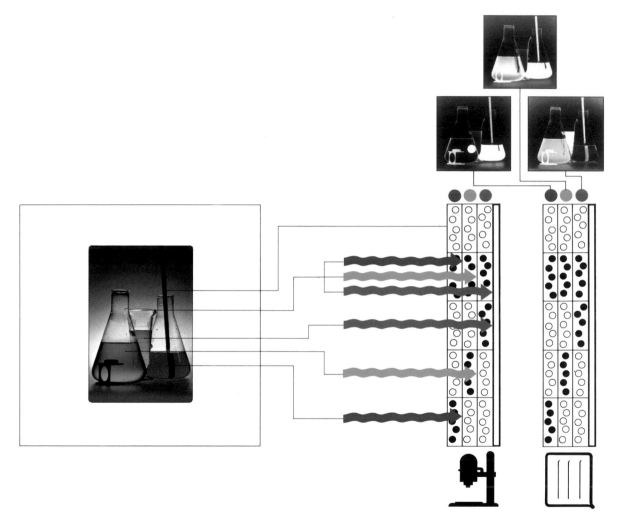

When the colored light from a slide (far left) in an enlarger falls on color reversal paper, each of the three primary colors (wavy lines) affects a different emulsion layer, one sensitive to red, another to blue and a third to green (colored dots above the paper cross section). Each color produces an invisible "latent" image (gray dots) in the layer sensitive to it. Where the slide is black, no light gets through and no latent image is formed in the paper. Where the slide is white all three primaries get through and all layers are exposed. During the first development (tray symbol) the three latent images are converted into silver negative images (top). The density of each negative depends on the amount of the corresponding primary color in the slide. For example, the dark silver areas of the red negative are a record of the red-colored areas of the subject.

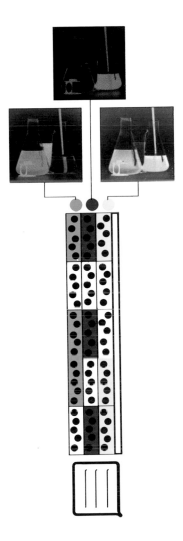

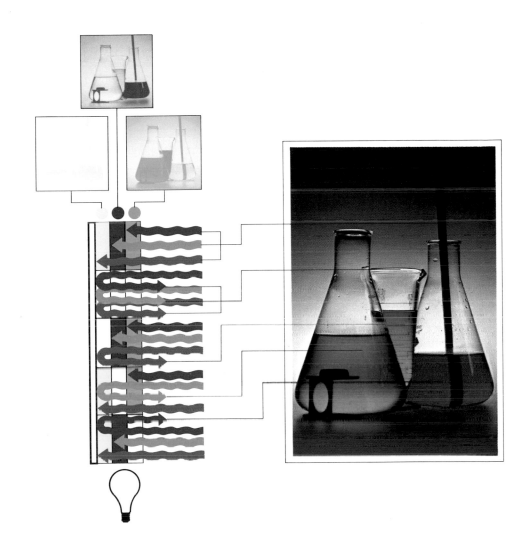

To convert negative silver images, generated by the steps shown at left, into positive color images requires the step diagramed above. First the emulsion is fogged in the second, or color, developer, making all emulsion not already developed susceptible to development. The chemicals in the bath then develop this emulsion and, as they do, change in a way that releases dyes. Since the amount of second development depends on how much emulsion was left undeveloped by the first development, the dye images are the reverse of the initial silver images—they are positives (top). In each layer the positive color is the complement of the color of the light first recorded there. Cyan dye is formed in the red-sensitive layer, magenta in the green-sensitive layer and yellow in the blue-sensitive layer (colored dots above the paper cross section).

The last step in producing a color print Is to bleach out all the silver in the three emulsion layers. This action leaves only positive color images in each layer (top). When white light—a mixture of colors (wavy lines)—shines on these three superimposed primary color images, each image subtracts its own color from the light reflected back to the viewer's eye. What is left (arrowheads) re-creates the original colors. The red of the subject, for example, has formed yellow and magenta images but no cyan. The yellow image subtracts the blue portion of the white light and the magenta subtracts the green, leaving only red to be reflected back to the eye of the viewer. Other colors are reproduced in the same way by combinations of dyes in the print. White appears where no color is subtracted from white light by a dye and black where all colors are subtracted.

Printing Negatives in Two Steps

Processing prints from color negatives can involve as little as two basic chemical baths—and those at room temperature—with some of the new systems for home color work. Most, like the Color by Beseler method demonstrated at right, can be used with any brand of either of the two types of printing paper, but be sure to buy chemicals suited to the paper—type A contains oil-based materials, type B water-based ones, and they need different solutions. Both types will give color of equal quality. In addition, some are resin-coated; they dry quickly without curling when hung on a line, but should not be dried in contact with a heated print dryer (the emulsion will be spotted).

Of all the new systems, the Beseler is quickest and easiest to use. Just mix the two solutions, following the instructions on the package, and pour them into brown bottles labeled Step 1 and Step 2. If the solutions are not warmed, processing requires 7 minutes for Step 1 and 2½ minutes for Step 2 (at a room temperature of 72°F.). The procedure can be speeded up by maintaining the temperature of the liquids at 107°F. while using them; Steps 1 and 2 then take only one minute each.

Processing can be carried out in two trays, but the kind of drum shown here is more convenient for two reasons: it permits working with the room lights on, and it also provides better agitation, which is essential for good results. Other equipment is standard except for the squeegee—many photographers find that an ordinary automobile windshield wiper works better than do most of the squeegees made specifically for photographic use.

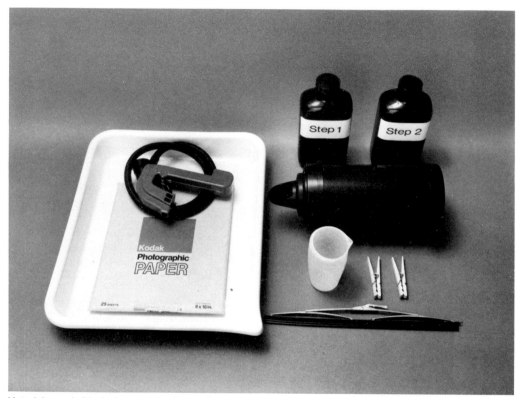

Materials needed include a washing tray and siphon, brown bottles for solutions, processing drum, four-ounce graduate, clothesline clips and a windshield wiper or other squeegee.

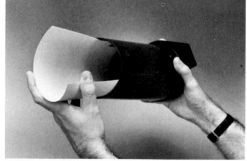

Expose a sheet of color print paper in the enlarger (room lights are out). Insert the paper into the processing drum, making sure the emulsion side is toward the center.

1

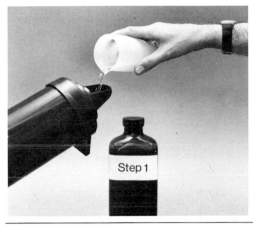

1 | Room lights may now be turned on. Pour Step 1 solution into the drum (left) to develop the image and agitate by rolling the drum (above). Empty Step 1 (right) and shake drum dry.

2

3

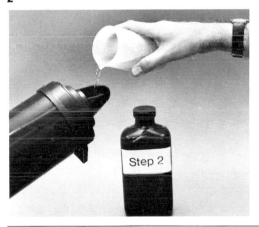

◄ 2 | Pour in Step 2 solution (left) to bleach out the developed silver and fix the dye images, following the procedure shown for Step 1. After pouring out the Step 2 solution, wash the drum. Caution: do not contaminate Step 1 with any Step 2.

3 | Wash the print—the time depends on the type ► —In a siphon tray as shown at right, or in the processing drum.

4

5

4 | Lay the print on a smooth clean surface and squeegee off as much water as possible. Treat the print gently; wet emulsion is easily damaged.

5 | Hang the print to dry. The blue tint of type A paper fades as it dries to the natural result shown in the right half of the picture at right.

A Personal Control over Color

Fred Pleasure's photographs of designs in rock, seaweed and water are the evidence that high-quality color prints can be made in the home darkroom with the new simplified color printing processes. Although the Beseler process used for these pictures is the simplest of the eight described on pages 190-191, it no less than the others can provide accurate color reproduction or versatile color control.

Pleasure's own technique adds an unusual wrinkle. He shoots the original pictures on slide film—for his imagery he prefers its tones and its fine grain to 35mm color negative film—and then converts the positive transparencies into color negatives with his enlarger. When he prints he controls exposure area by area. Pleasure strives for faithful copying of the transparency, and does not modify his colors. His method, however, can be used to modify color in a simple way at the negative-making stage. At this point, the color control can be direct: to add more blue, for example, a blue filter is placed in the enlarger—deeper for deeper blue, lighter for lighter blue. Such direct adjustments are easier to gauge visually than the indirect complementary color balancing required at the printmaking stage; then a deeper blue result would call for a darker yellow filter. (Although complementary color filters must still be used when the final print is made, they can be the standardized "normal" set specified on the paper box; some of the usual trial-and-error tests can be skipped, leaving the photographer free to work on spot control of exposure, since color balance has already been achieved in the negative.)

Traprock on Route 44, West Hartford, Connecticut

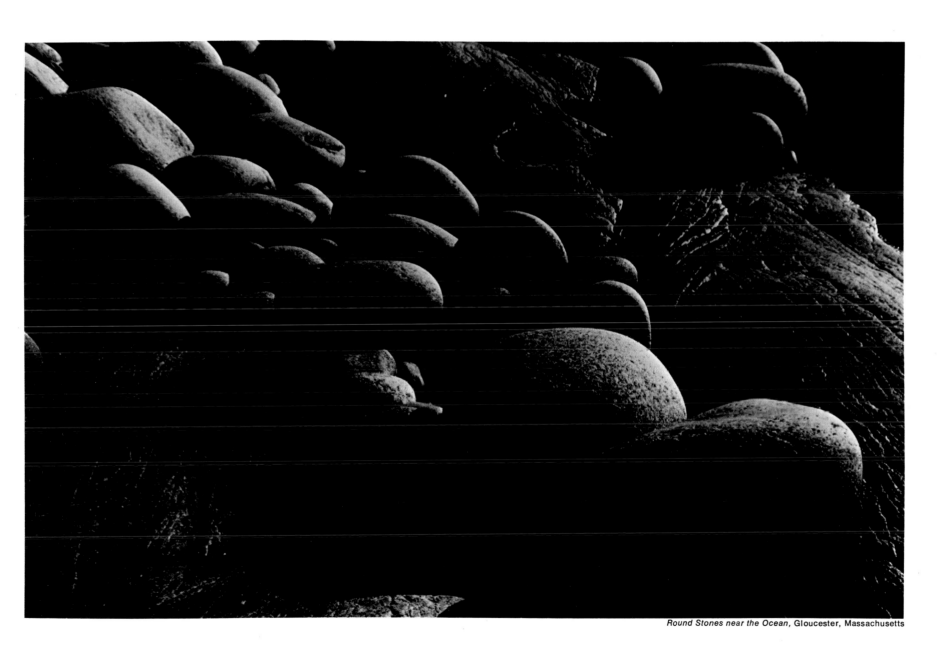

Round Stones near the Ocean, Gloucester, Massachusetts

◄ *The low contrast in this scene permitted Pleasure to adjust exposure for the soft highlight areas, recording their detail without seriously underexposing the rest of the image.*

In printing this ultra-contrasty scene, Pleasure gave extra exposure to some areas to bring out detail in the highlights of those rocks struck by the slanting rays of the early sun.

197

Rock, Water and Yellow Seaweed, Gloucester, Massachusetts

*The exposure of the original slide accurately
caught the small areas of brilliant yellow and red
in this scene, but the central round rock was
overexposed and thus lacked detail. To remedy
that, it was burned in during printing.*

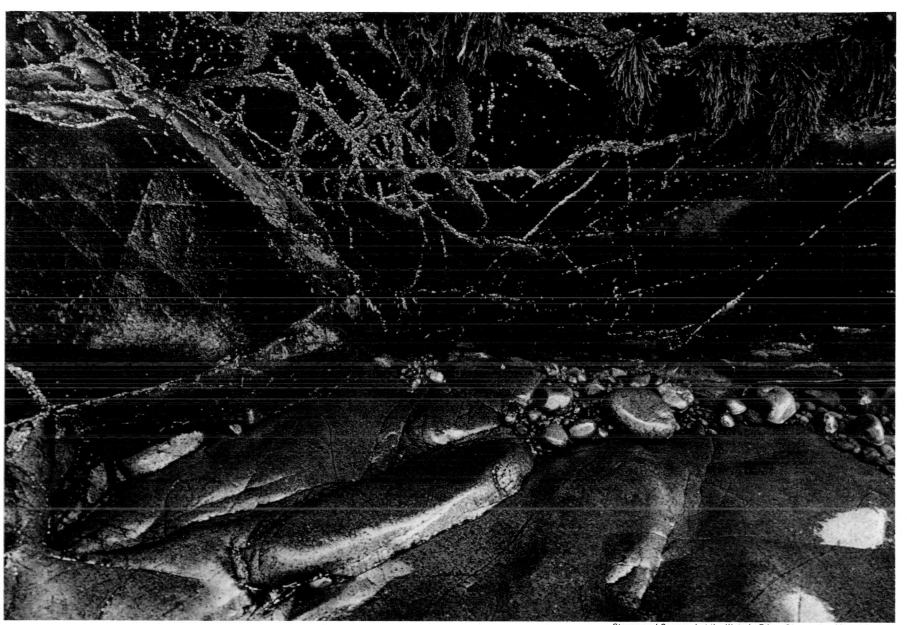

Stones and Seaweed at the Water's Edge, Gloucester, Massachusetts

Pleasure aimed for detail in the dark seaweed in
this picture, and he gauged exposure on that area.
As a result the bright bottom portion was
overexposed in the slide; like the picture opposite
it was burned in to bring up detail.

1973 Cameras and Lenses

Although in 1973 there was no international photographic exposition such as Photokina, with its dramatic presentation of advances in camera design, a surprising number of new camera models were marketed. Twenty-nine of these are described on this and the following three pages.

Most new SLRs have automatic exposure control that requires manual setting of shutter speed, leaving the control mechanism to use the information from the light meter to set lens aperture automatically. Some SLRs, however, such as the Pentax ES II, use the opposite method, with the shutter speed automatically set.

Among new rangefinder cameras, the Olympus SPN is unique in offering a choice of metering: exposure is averaged for the whole scene or individualized for a center spot, in addition to manual control. The Fujica GM670 and GL690 are the first larger-than-35mm cameras to have automatic exposure control (page 208). The meter system is built into the new AE lenses, rather than into the camera body.

The Keystone cameras occupy an unusual place in the roster of new models; they are the only picture-in-one-minute cameras on the market besides the Polaroid Land cameras. The Keystone 850 will accept several Polaroid Land film sizes, either black and white or color, square or rectangular.

Single Lens Reflex Cameras

manufacturer model	price[1]	standard lens and mount	size	light meter	shutter speeds	other features
GAF L-17	$250	55mm f/1.7 Auto Chinon, Pentax screw	35mm	averaging	1-1/1000	manual control of meter needle
Canon FTbn	available in Japan 1973, in U.S. 1974	sold separately	35mm	spot	1-1/1000	manual control of meter needle; exposure measured at full aperture
Topcon IC-1	289	50mm f/2 HI-Topcor, Topcon bayonet	35mm	center-weighted, automatically sets aperture	1-1/500	exposure measured at full aperture
Konica Autoreflex A-1000	330	52mm f/1.8 Auto Hexanon, Konica bayonet	35mm	center-weighted, automatically sets aperture	1-1/1000	exposure measured at full aperture
Asahi Pentax Spotmatic F	not sold in U.S.	50mm f/1.4 SMC Takumar, Pentax screw	35mm	center-weighted	1-1/1000	manual control of meter needle; exposure measured at full aperture
Honeywell Pentax Spotmatic F	379	55mm f/1.8 SMC Takumar, Pentax screw	35mm	center-weighted	1-1/1000	manual control of meter needle; exposure measured at full aperture
Canon EF	available in Japan 1973, in U.S. 1974	50mm f/1.4 Canon, Canon breech lock	35mm	enlarged spot, automatically sets aperture	30-1/1000	exposure measured at full aperture
Bell & Howell FD 35	325	50mm f/1.8 Bell & Howell/Canon, Canon breech lock	35mm	center-weighted	1-1/500	manual control of meter needle; exposure measured at full aperture
Olympus OM-1	425	50mm f/1.8 Zuiko, Olympus OM bayonet	35mm	center-weighted	1-1/1000	lightest SLR; manual control of meter needle; exposure measured at full aperture; 12 viewing screens available
Minolta SF-T 102	445	50mm f/1.4 MC Rokkor-X, Minolta bayonet	35mm	partially weighted	1-1/1000	meter compensates for high contrast areas; manual control of meter needle; exposure measured at full aperture

Minolta XK

Kowa Six II

manufacturer model	price[1]	standard lens and mount	size	light meter	shutter speeds	other features
Konica Autoreflex T3	$460	50mm f/1.7 Auto Hexanon, Konica bayonet	35mm	center-weighted, automatically sets aperture	1-1/1000	hair-trigger shutter release; exposure measured at full aperture
Asahi Pentax ES II	not sold in U.S.	50mm f/1.4 SMC Takumar, Pentax screw	35mm	center-weighted, automatically sets shutter	8-1/1000	electronically controlled shutter; exposure measured at full aperture
Honeywell Pentax ES II	600	55mm f/1.8 SMC Takumar, Pentax screw	35mm	center-weighted, automatically sets shutter	8-1/1000	electronically controlled shutter; exposure measured at full aperture
Kowa Six MM	650	85mm f/2.8 Kowa S, Kowa breech lock	2¼ x 2¼	none	1-1/500	between-the-lens shutter; viewfinder with meter available; interchangeable back
Kowa Six II	available in Japan 1973, in U.S. 1974	85mm f/2.8 Kowa S, Kowa breech lock	2¼ x 2¼	none	1-1/500	between-the-lens shutter; interchangeable back needs no film shield; viewfinder with meter available
Alpha 11 el	699	sold separately	35mm	center-weighted	1-1/1000	completely die-cast body; full or ½ frame sizes available; signal lights indicate exposure; electronic, shockproof exposure meter; 4 different focusing methods on same screen
Minolta XK	700	50mm f/1.7 MC Rokkor-X, Minolta bayonet	35mm	partially weighted averaging	16-1/2000	meter compensates for high-contrast areas; manual control of needle; 9 different viewing screens and 5 different viewfinders available
Topcon Super DM	727	50mm f/1.4 REGN Topcor-M, Topcon bayonet	35mm	center-weighted	1-1/1000	motorized film advance; manual control of meter needle; exposure measured at full aperture

[1] Manufacturers' approximate suggested price at the end of 1973.

Konica Auto S3

Yashica Electro 35 FC

Rangefinder Cameras

manufacturer model	price[1]	standard lens	size	light meter	shutter speeds	other features
Petri 7sII	$90	45mm f/2.8 Petri	35mm	averaging	1-1/500	also available with f/1.8 lens at $105; manual control of meter needle
Yashica 35 ME	95	38mm f/2.8 Yashinon	35mm	center-weighted, automatically sets shutter and aperture	1/30-1/650	compact size; available in black finish at $100
Fujica GEr	available in Japan 1973, In U.S. 1974	38mm f/2.8 Seiko	35mm	averaging, automatically sets shutter and aperture	4-1/800	
Yashica Electro 35 FC	available in Japan 1973, in U.S. 1974	40mm f/2.8 Yashinon	35mm	center-weighted, automatically sets shutter and aperture	4-1/1000	
Yashica Electro 35 GSN	165	45mm f/1.7 Yashinon DX	35mm	center-weighted, automatically sets shutter and aperture	30-1/500	available in black finish (GTN) at $180
Olympus 35 SPN	170	42mm f/1.7 Zuiko	35mm	averaging and spot automatically sets shutter and aperture	1-1/500	manual override of exposure controls
Konica Auto S3	185	38mm f/1.8 Hexanon	35mm	center-weighted, automatically sets aperture	1/8-1/500	manual control of shutter speed with manual override of aperture setting; special outdoor flash control
Leica CL 35	597	40mm f/2 Summicron-C	35mm	enlarged spot	1/2-1/1000	very compact; automatic parallax correction; through-the-lens meter; takes many Leitz bayonet-mount lenses; manual control of meter needle

Sinar I

Keystone 60-Second Everflash 850

Other Cameras

manufacturer model	price[1]	standard lens	size	shutter speeds	other features
Keystone 60-Second Everflash 850	$100	115mm f/8.8	Polaroid Land Film 107, 108 or 88	10-1/500	takes Polaroid Land black-and-white or Polacolor film, square or rectangular. Battery-operated, automatic exposure control; built-in flash
Rollei A26	200	40mm f/3.5 Zeiss Sonnar	126 cartridge	1/30-1/250	very compact; push-pull film advance; fully automatic light meter; electronic flash unit accessory
Sinar f	395	sold separately	4 x 5	varies with lens and accessories	very light (6 lbs., 6½ oz. without lens) view camera; yaw-free swing and tilt

[1] Manufacturers' approximate suggested price at the end of 1973.

Lenses for 35mm Cameras

The charts on these pages, listing 60 lenses introduced in 1973, show trends toward sharpness and versatility. Most noticeable is an improvement on an old technique for reducing lens-surface reflections, which can be blocked by coating the glass with a thin—about one forty thousandth of a millimeter —layer of such compounds as magnesium fluoride. Single layers on outer lens surfaces are not new, but multiple layers on all or most elements in a lens work better, and in 1973 most manufacturers swung to "multicoating."

Greater flexibility increased control over image size. The Vivitar Series I f/3.5 zoom, one of a group of computer-designed lenses, has a range of 70mm to 210mm and focuses to 11½ inches. Other zoom lenses span the range from wide-angle to long lens. Perhaps most unusual is a Canon lens that both tilts and shifts to give a 35mm SLR view camera control *(page 206).*

	manufacturer and model	price[1]	focal length and speed	antiflare coating	mounts
very wide angle and fisheye lenses (15mm to 20mm)	Auto Nikkor	$1,100	15mm f/5.6	multiple	Nikon bayonet
	Canon FD	500	15mm f/2.8 fisheye	multiple	most Canon cameras
	Auto Nikkor	500	16mm f/3.5 fisheye	multiple	Nikon bayonet
	Fujinon F/EBC	475	16mm f/2.5 fisheye	multiple	Pentax screw
	Soligor	275	17mm f/4	standard	Pentax screw, Nikon and Minolta bayonets
	Auto Miranda	275	17mm f/4	standard	Miranda bayonet
	Yashinon DS	325	20mm f/3.3	standard	most screw-mount SLRs
wide angle lenses (21mm to 30mm)	Petri Auto	250	21mm f/4	standard	Petri breech lock
	Auto Hexanon	275	24mm f/2.8	standard	Konica automatic bayonet
	Auto Miranda EE	200	25mm f/2.8	standard	Miranda Auto Sensorex EE camera
	Soligor	175	25mm f/2.8	standard	Miranda Sensorex EE camera
	Soligor	150	28mm f/2.8	standard	Miranda Sensorex EE camera
	Zeiss F-Distagon	1,700	30mm f/3.5	multiple	Rollei SL66 and Hasselblad 500 C and EL series cameras
medium wide angle lenses (35mm)	Alpex Automatic	price unavailable	35mm f/2.8	standard	Pentax screw, Nikon and Minolta bayonets
	Bushnell	100	35mm f/2.8	standard	mounts for most SLRs
	Canon TS	625	35mm f/2.8 with perspective control, tilt	multiple	Canon F-1, FTb and TLb cameras
	Fujinon EBC	175	35mm f/2.8	multiple	Pentax screw
	Soligor	125	35mm f/2.8	standard	Miranda Sensorex EE camera
	Vivitar	175	35mm f/1.9	standard	mounts for most SLRs
	Auto Nikkor	475	35mm f/1.4	multiple	Nikon bayonet
normal lenses (40mm to 57mm)	Summicron-C (Leitz)	250	40mm f/2	standard	Leica CL camera
	Canon FD	250	50mm f/3.5 macro	multiple	most Canon cameras
	Schneider SL-Xenon	75	50mm f/1.8	standard	Rollei SL35 camera
	Rokkor-X	100	50mm f/1.7	multiple	Minolta bayonet for Minolta SR cameras
	Rokkor-X	150	50mm f/1.4	multiple	Minolta bayonet for Minolta SR cameras
	Zeiss HFT-Planar	175	50mm f/1.4	multiple	Rollei SL35 camera
	Fujinon EBC	225	55mm f/3.5 macro	multiple	Pentax screw
	Miranda	225	55mm f/3.5 macro	standard	Miranda bayonet
	Canon FD	275	55mm f/1.2	multiple	most Canon cameras
	Auto Hexanon	250	57mm f/1.2	standard	Konica automatic bayonet

Auto Nikkor 15mm f/5.6

Zeiss Tele-Tessar 350mm f/5.6

	manufacturer and model	price[1]	focal length and speed	antiflare coating	mounts
medium long lenses (85 mm to 105mm)	Spiratone	$ 100	85mm f/1.8	standard	mounts for most SLRs; adapters for others
	Takumar SMC	250	85mm f/1.8	multiple	Pentax screw
	Elmar-C (Leitz)	275	90mm f/1.4	standard	Leica CL camera
	Takumar SMC	175	100mm f/4 macro	multiple	Pentax screw
	Rokkor-X	400	100mm f/3.5 macro	multiple	Minolta bayonet for Minolta SR cameras
	Auto Hexanon	175	105mm f/4 macro	standard	Konica automatic bayonet
	Soligor	125	105mm f/2.8	standard	Miranda Sensorex EE camera
long lenses (135mm)	Takumar SMC	350	135mm f/4 macro	multiple	Pentax screw
	Fujinon EBC	175	135mm f/3.5	multiple	Pentax screw
	Schneider Tele-Xenar	200	135mm f/3.5	standard	Rollei SL 35 camera
	Bushnell	125	135mm f/2.8	standard	mounts for most SLRs
	Vivitar Auto Telephoto Series 1	175	135mm f/2.3	standard	mounts for most SLRs
	Spiratone	125	135mm f/1.8	standard	mounts for most SLRs; adapters for others
very long lenses (200mm and up)	Vivitar Auto Telephoto Series 1	210	200mm f/3	standard	mounts for most SLRs
	Soligor	175	300mm f/5.6	standard	Miranda bayonet
	Zeiss Tele-Tessar	1,200	350mm f/5.6	multiple	Hasselblad 500 C and EL series cameras
	Fujinon EBC	600	400mm f/4.5	multiple	Pentax screw
	Auto Nikkor	675	400mm f/4.5	multiple	Nikon bayonet
	Yashinon DX	400	500mm f/8 mirror	standard	most screw mount SLRs
	Fujinon EBC	800	600mm f/5.6	multiple	Pentax screw
	Lumetar	650	1250mm f/10 mirror	standard	T adapters for most SLRs
zoom lenses	Canon FD	price unavailable	35-70mm f/2.8	multiple	most Canon cameras
	Auto Hexanon	700	35-100mm f/2.8	multiple	Konica automatic bayonet
	Tamron	600	38-100mm f/3.5	multiple	most bayonet mount SLRs; adapters for others
	Petri Auto	300	45-135mm f/3.5	standard	Petri breech lock
	Fujinon EBC	700	54-270mm f/4.5	multiple	Pentax screw
	Vivitar Auto Series 1	375	70-210mm f/3.5	standard	mounts for most SLRs
	Fujinon EBC	400	75-150mm f/4.5	multiple	Pentax screw
	Soligor C/D	275	80-200mm f/3.5	standard	mounts for most SLRs
	Takumar SMC	2,000	135-600mm f/6.7	multiple	Pentax screw

[1] Manufacturers' approximate suggested price at the end of 1973.

Three Cameras from Rollei

Something new, something old and something very small will be added to the line of cameras made by Rollei, the West German firm that transferred much of its production to Singapore (PHOTOGRAPHY YEAR 1973).

Something new is the SLX 66, a 2¼ x 2¼ SLR designed to give press photographers very rapid picture taking—as many as 20 exposures can be made in a second. This speed comes from all-electric operation employing a "linear" motor—one with its essential parts spread in a flattened ring instead of wound in bulky coils. Twin rotors, circling the interior of the lens, not only respond to an exposure meter to set aperture but also cock and release the shutter electrically without intervening gears or couplers.

Something very small is a prototype for a projected group of pocket-sized cameras using the very small 110-size film introduced in 1972. It is about a third smaller than the smallest 110-size camera previously available.

Something old is the distinguished Voigtländer name, revived after a two-year hiatus by Rollei. It appears on three 35mm cameras: an SLR called the VSL 1 and two rangefinder cameras, the VF 101 and VF 102, identical except that the VF 102 *(above, left)* accepts a 40mm f/2.8 or an 80mm f/3.5 lens, interchangeably.

A Movable Lens

A wide-angle lens that shifts in any direction and even tilts was marketed in 1973. An improved PC—for perspective control—lens, it brings to 35mm SLR cameras optical versatility once limited to bulky view cameras.

Reborn Voigtländer, the VF 102

The new lens, like earlier versions, moves up, down, sideways and at angles to control apparent perspective —the tops or sides of objects will not converge when the camera is angled. (Alternatively they can be made to converge more sharply than they ordinarily would.) The new feature is tilt. Tilting creates an optical relationship between lens and film plane that permits great depth of field, maintaining sharp focus at almost every point in the image. The 35mm f/2.5 lens, made by Canon for all its current 35mm SLRs, costs $630.

Canon TS 35mm f/2.8 with Shift and Tilt

Tiny Rollei A 110 and All-electronic Rolleiflex SLX 66

Sending Photos by Laser Beam

A system that uses laser beams to send photographs over telephone lines began extensive trials by the Associated Press in 1973. Called Laserphoto, it transmits pictures four times faster than the present AP Wirephoto, without need for the chemical processing now employed, and it is expected to become the wire agency's prime method of distributing pictures to some 4,500 clients by 1976.

The heart of the new system is a safe, helium-neon laser that emits a narrow, concentrated beam of red light at very low wattage—less than 1/1000 watt. The beam scans a photograph 100 times per inch of surface area. Light-sensitive cells pick up the beam's reflected light and convert it into electric currents whose strength depends on the brightness of the reflected light. In this way the image's shades of gray are coded for transmission to receivers in the newsrooms of AP clients.

The receiving machine sends the current into another helium-neon laser, controlling the strength of the light beam it generates. This beam is di-

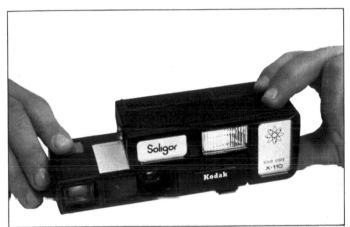
Electronic Flash for Pocket Camera

rected onto an oscillating mirror that reflects it across dry, light-sensitive paper, scanning back and forth in the same pattern used for transmission. As the beam scans the paper, it passes the picture information onto its surface. After developing (by means of a heat roller), a glossy photograph appears that is identical to the original.

Cure for Red-eyed Pictures
Users of many small, instant-loading cameras and some larger ones as well have been startled by color close-ups shot with flash: often the subjects come out with red eyes. One new way to return the red eyes to their natural color—a compact, horizontal electronic flash—was introduced in 1973. Another way, a rigid plastic rod that extends any flashcube or magicube mounting, was also recommended by some of the major camera makers.

The red-eyed look was caused by the frequent location of the flash shoe at a point just above the lens. From this position light from the flash shone straight through the pupil of the subject's eye to illuminate the network of blood ves-

sels exposed in the back of the eye's interior—which the lens thereupon recorded in its healthy rich red.

The horizontal flash unit that is shown above costs about $25, and solves the problem by moving the light source well to one side to illuminate the eyes of the subject at an angle. Any light that enters and is reflected back out misses the camera lens, so that none of the eye's interior, only its exterior, is recorded on film. That way, baby's big blue eyes come out blue, as expected, and not red.

Lightweight Long Lens
The lightest lens yet for its length, Honeywell's new 1,250mm Lumetar f/10 lens *(chart pages 204-205)* weighs just three and three quarter pounds. It utilizes two curved mirrors and a single, thin lens instead of multiple lens elements to achieve its great focal length, and it can be used not only to make distant objects seem near but also to produce very large pictures of objects not so far off—it focuses as close as 16 feet. Despite its light weight and compact size—13 inches long, 5½ inches in diameter—it is best used with a tripod, since the extremely long focal length greatly magnifies camera movement.

A Compact Leica
During the half-century since the Leica camera brought about a revolution in photography with the first compact, high-quality 35mm camera, succeeding models have grown progressively larger. In 1973, the manufacturer reverted to its original idea and placed on the market the smallest and lightest Leica that has been sold in decades (see charts listing specifications of new

cameras, pages 200-203). Even more surprising, this Leica—a name that has always seemed synonymous with Germany—was manufactured in Japan. The little camera is the first result of a real collaboration between the Leica's originator, Leitz, and the Minolta firm of Japan (see PHOTOGRAPHY YEAR 1973): the camera body is made in the Far East, then returned to the parent plant in Germany to be checked.

The new rangefinder camera, measuring just 4¾ x 3 x 1¼ inches and weighing about 20 ounces with a 40mm lens attached, is called the Leica CL, the initials standing for compact light-measuring. It has, as do other cameras in the Leica family, a semiautomatic through-the-lens light metering system. When the film is advanced, a cadmium-sulfide cell on a pivot arm swings into position behind the lens; just before the shutter opens, a spring activated by the release button quickly pulls the meter cell out of the way.

The Leica CL is equipped to take a wide range of Leitz lenses. Two, made

Tiny Leica CL

specially for this compact camera of 40mm and 90mm focal lengths, are designed to be focused directly by the coupled rangefinder without any need for special adapters.

Where the Camera Bargains Are

In years past photographers who wanted to save money when they bought cameras and lenses often waited until they could travel to Japan or Germany or to a free port such as Shannon in Ireland, Freeport in the Bahamas or Hong Kong, where no import duty is charged. With worldwide currency fluctuations and changes in trade practices those bargains have disappeared, a PHOTOGRAPHY YEAR survey shows.

To be sure, list prices abroad still seemed lower than U.S. prices in 1973. Japanese cameras sold in Japan for just over half their U.S. list cost. In freeport stores checked by PHOTO YEAR correspondents, prices were 15 to 30 per cent of list figures in the charts. But the charts specify manufacturers' suggested list prices, which are heavily discounted in the U.S. Actual prices charged by some American dealers, reporters found, were as much as 50 per cent below list. A buyer, shopping bigcity stores or mail-order houses, could do about as well in the U.S. as in the manufacturers' home country—and probably better than in a free port.

Automatic Exposure for Hasselblad

The growing popularity of automatic exposure controls among professionals was underlined by Zeiss plans for a unit to fit lenses for the costly Hasselblad 2¼ x 2¼ SLR. The device, to be available in 1974, will control aperture but will also permit manual settings.

2¼ x 2¾ Fujica GM670 with Automatic Exposure

Automatic Exposure with Big Negatives

Two Fujica rangefinder cameras introduced in Japan but not sold elsewhere in 1973 are the first to offer automatic exposure control for negatives larger than the 35mm size. The Fujica GM670, with a 2¼ x 2¾-inch format, and the Fujica GL690, with a 2¼ x 3¼-inch format —easy-to-enlarge sizes popular among professionals specializing in weddings and party coverage—both use the new Fujinon AE lens that has an exposure meter mounted on it *(above)* and is coupled to an electronically controlled shutter. The meter automatically selects the shutter speed—from 8 to 1/500 second—for correct exposure with a preselected f-stop.

Finer Grain Film for Pocket Cameras

An improved version of the color print film made for the Kodak Pocket Instamatic 110 size cameras was introduced early in 1973 to give even sharper pictures from the tiny negatives. The new film has a grain even finer than its very fine-grain predecessor, and it also remains fresh longer. The speed remains the same, at ASA 80.

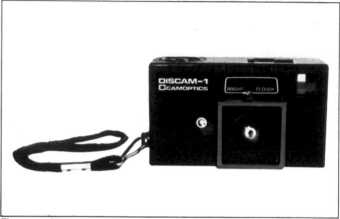

Throwaway Discam-1

The Disposable Camera

First aid for the forgetful photographer who leaves his camera at home was offered by Camoptics Limited of Hong Kong: a "disposable" factory-loaded camera with enough 35mm color film for 20 pictures, sold as a complete unit at film counters.

When the photographer has used all the film, he returns the entire camera and gets back only his processed pictures; the camera is reloaded and sold again. After a few such cycles the manufacturer throws the camera out. Called the Discam-1, the camera has a fixed-focus lens, a single shutter speed and an adapter for a flash attachment.

Big Zoom

An ultralong zoom lens went into limited production late in 1973. Asahi Optical of Japan designed a Takumar lens with a range of 135mm, the most popular telephoto length, to 600mm, longer than any zoom for 35mm SLRs on the market today. A spokesman said the lens had a speed of f/6.7 and multiple antiflare coating. Its optical parts consist of 15 elements in 12 groups.

Roundup

Every year brings with it a potpourri of photographic events, some of them promising, some of them marking the end of an era. Into the last category for 1973 falls the death of Edward Steichen (opposite), the long-lived giant of modern photography, who not only touched but left his mark upon virtually every facet of the medium for nearly three quarters of a century. No other figure in photographic history covered such a span, either in time or in style and substance. But the year also saw the end of the careers of such notable photographers as Dean Brown, Eliot Elisofon, Stan Wayman and Ugo Mulas.

Among the happier events of 1973 were the opening of a new photographic hall at the Smithsonian Institution in Washington; the inclusion of the art of photography in high-school curricula; and the salvaging in London of a unique collection of 19th Century portraits. Looking ahead, a list of some of the photographic events scheduled for 1974 appears on page 236.

With a gaze that faltered no less before ▶ the camera than when he stood behind it, the photographer Edward Steichen sat for his portrait many times throughout his life. When he was about seven, an anonymous 1880s photographer recorded his image in a Michigan village studio (top); in his nineties he sat for his colleague Yousuf Karsh (bottom right).

Steichen: The Versatile Master

During the last years of Edward Steichen's life (he died in March 1973, just two days before his 94th birthday), the grand old man of photography spent his mornings in the light-filled living room of his house in rural Connecticut. From his chair by the window he could look across a lily-covered pond to the white blossoms of a shad-blow tree—a frequent subject of his last photographs. His constant companion was Tripod, a comparably ancient three-legged dog, and close at hand were the keepsakes and memorabilia of the half century that had led him from one triumph to another through nearly every new development in photography.

In the late 1890s, when Steichen began his career, professional photography did not exist as it does today. There were portrait photographers and photographers of souvenir views, but the many other roles filled today were yet to come, some from Steichen himself. The most celebrated photographs were self-conscious attempts at pure art, many of them created by talented amateurs, who showed their work in the photographic salons held in London, Paris and Washington, D.C. This world was unknown to Steichen, who was then a lithographer's teen-age assistant in Milwaukee, but he shared its goals: to make photographs that would rival the paintings of Whistler and the Impressionists, and thus prove that photography was indeed a fine art. On weekends he took his camera out to the woods at the end of the trolley line in search of suitable subjects.

"The woods had moods," he later recalled, "and the moods aroused emotional reactions that I tried to render in photographs." He particularly liked the romantic effect of tree forms dissolved in mist or fading light. By trial and error he learned to throw the subject out of focus, to wet his lens or to jog the camera just at the moment of exposure, and thus get a soft image that transformed an ordinary wooded lot on the outskirts of Milwaukee into a realm of sylvan magic.

Steichen's early woodland scenes were among the best ever photographed. In them he fully realized his gift for romanticizing reality—a gift he was to retain throughout this career—and when he sent them off to the photographic salons their excellence was quickly acknowledged. Before he was 22, Steichen was internationally recognized as one of the leading pictorial photographers. This early success was not an accident. In addition to talent, Steichen had self-confidence and perseverance; he never doubted throughout his life that he could do whatever he wanted to.

His career in photography gained added luster following two years of painting in Paris. While there he photographed Rodin and many other leading artists and writers, and when he returned to New York in 1902 he set up shop on Fifth Avenue as a portrait photographer. It was during these years that he made the dramatic portrait of J. Pierpont Morgan that remains to

Out of the Stygian darkness financier J. Pierpont ▶ Morgan glares angrily into the camera. He is impeccably dressed in winged collar and ascot, and a gold watch chain loops across his sober vest. But one hand firmly grasps the arm of his chair, which a trick of light has transformed into a dagger thrust out at the spectator.

A "masterpiece," said Stieglitz of "The Pool —Evening," one of a group of pictures he bought from Steichen at their first meeting in 1900.

this day the archetypical image of the super-respectable robber baron. Steichen's pictures of notables pleased patrons and esthetes alike, and he began to enjoy that rarest and most delightful form of success, a *succès d'estime* that is also a commercial success. Alfred Stieglitz, a contemporary and photographic authority, considered him the greatest of all the Photo-Secessionists, the choice band of pictorialists that Stieglitz considered to be the most accomplished in the world. He often published Steichen's pictures in the Photo-Secessionist journal, *Camera Work*. Steichen's fame as a portraitist became so great that he had to move into larger quarters, and when he did, he made a fateful suggestion. He persuaded Stieglitz to take over his old studio at 291 Fifth Avenue and turn it into a gallery that would show photographs on an equal basis with drawings, paintings and sculpture. Thus would the artistic nature of photography be understood. Naturally, Steichen himself was an early exhibitor at the studio gallery, and when he returned to Paris in 1906 to resume his career as a painter he chose works of Rodin, Brancusi, Matisse, Picasso and other painters and sculptors whose exhibits at the new gallery gave Americans some of their first hints of the revolutionary changes of modern art.

As the spirit of Whistler and the Impressionists was superseded at the 291 gallery by the bold experiments of these other artists, Steichen became disenchanted with attempts to imitate paintings in photographs. He repudiated the old soft-focus approach in favor of sharp focus and unmanipulated printing in order to take full advantage of the medium's natural capacities. Steichen's growing interest in such "pure" as opposed to "pictorial" photography was strengthened when he got a job organizing aerial reconnaissance photography for the U.S. Army during World War I. In this work the most accurate representation was of the utmost importance. If a reconnaissance photograph could not be read, it was useless. This effort took him ever further from the impressionistic approach to photography, and after the war he set out to master the new approach by an unusual method: he photographed a single cup and saucer more than 1,000 times.

While Steichen was blazing the artistic trail photography would follow for decades to come, he was also continuing to explore new areas of use. He was fascinated by the growing possibilities of photography in the mass media. He saw that large-circulation magazines would bring photography to many more people than could ever be reached by salons, museums and little magazines like *Camera Work*. But he wanted mass-media photography to be good, and in 1923 he went to New York and got a job as principal photographer for Condé Nast's smart new magazine, *Vanity Fair.*

The idea of producing pictures to order for a commercial client troubled many serious photographers. But not Steichen. "Art for art's sake" is dead, he later asserted—if indeed it had ever existed. "There never has been a period when the best thing we had was not commercial art." He maintained that, from the dawn of civilization, the artist has usually been "what we might call a glorified press agent." He explained his position to his poet brother-in-law Carl Sandburg, "If my technic, imagination and vision is any good, I ought to be able to put the best values of my non-commercial and experimental photography into a pair of shoes, a tube of tooth paste, a jar of face cream, a mattress or any object that I want to light up and make humanly interesting in the advertising photograph. . . . If I can't express the best that's in me through . . . advertising photographs . . . then I'm no good."

The issue was fairly joined, and it has not been resolved to everyone's satisfaction to this day. Many photographers still make a sharp division between the work they do for a living and the work they do for themselves. Steichen, however, tried to make the two one. For *Vanity Fair* he made a brilliant series of portraits that captured the glamour of actors, writers and other personalities in the public eye. Some of these pictures—for example the portraits of Charles Laughton, Greta Garbo and Paul Robeson—remain classic images of these performers. Steichen also devised many ingenious solutions to the problem of making fashion photographs look new and different, and some of these pictures joined his portraits in museums.

He was not always so successful with his advertising photographs, but even here he was sometimes able to express the best that was in him in photographs such as *Peeling Potatoes,* one of a series he made for a hand-lotion firm. The subject is simple enough: a close-up view of a bowl full of potatoes and the sturdy hands of a housewife. But the approach is far more convincing than the usual diamond-encrusted cosmetics ad. These are, or appear to be, the real hands of a woman who does her own housework, and they have the simple, four-square dignity of a good documentary.

Through photographs like these Steichen contributed greatly to raising the artistic standards of commercial photography, and the high fees he asked for and got (he was said at one time to be the highest-paid photographer in the world) helped make magazine photography the remunerative profession it became. In the end, however, even he grew tired. The work became routine and boring, and after 15 years of great success Steichen retired from commercial photography.

Although Steichen's great work as a photographer ended, he still had ahead of him one of the most significant roles of his life. The outbreak of World War II found him restless in his retirement, and despite his age, 62, he persuaded the U.S. Navy to let him organize a photographic task force to document the Navy's part in the war. His own photographs of the war, though

214

The air of bored disdain caught in Steichen's 1935 portrait of Charles Laughton seems so perfectly in character that there is no way of telling whether it represents an assumed role or the true man—a tribute to the artistic genius of both the actor and the photographer.

In his inaugural effort as an advertising photographer, Steichen promoted a hand lotion by making the kitchen drudgery of peeling potatoes seem almost palpable. Although the hands belonged to the wife of the advertising agency's president, Steichen later remarked, "I could tell by the way she cut the potatoes that this wasn't the first time she had done it."

effective, lacked the devastating power of the work of such younger photographers as Robert Capa, Eugene Smith and David Douglas Duncan. He was too much of a romantic to photograph war. However, during and after World War II, he organized two exhibitions of war photographs that led to his embarking in 1947 on a new career as Director of Photography of New York's Museum of Modern Art.

Since its founding in 1929, The Museum of Modern Art has always recognized photography as an art. But under Steichen's direction the museum's photography collection was enlarged and diversified to include commercial as well as art and documentary photography. He also organized 44 exhibitions covering all types of photography from abstract to documentary, introducing many young photographers to the public.

The most famous exhibition, and in some ways the crowning achievement of Steichen's life, was "The Family of Man," which opened at the Modern in January 1955 and went on to become the most popular photography exhibition ever assembled. Steichen himself traced the origin of this show to his mother's lessons in tolerance. But its more immediate roots lay in Steichen's own experience of the waste and destructiveness of two world wars. "What was needed," he later recalled, "was a positive statement on what a wonderful thing life was, how marvelous people were, and above all, how alike people were in all parts of the world."

Steichen called upon photographers from all over the world to assist him in creating The Family of Man. Over two million photographs were viewed, and out of them 503 pictures from 68 countries were chosen. The result was a diverse and moving picture of the variety in unity of mankind such as only great collaboration could produce, and although it hardly put an end to war —only a romantic like Steichen could have hoped it might—it was a great success by ordinary standards. It was seen not just by museumgoers in New York but by ordinary people in Japan, India, Europe—even by barefooted Indians in Guatemala.

When Steichen finally left active work behind him, he had mastered not one but a half dozen careers, each illustrious enough to satisfy a lesser man. He had led artists in exploiting two quite different styles, popularized not only serious photography but also the great modern movement in painting and sculpture, made memorable portraits, practically invented fashion and advertising photography, and finally, assembled the most memorable exhibit of photographs yet seen. Yet he never entirely stopped. In his nineties in Connecticut, he persisted in photographing his little shad-blow tree —quiet, unassuming pictures that somehow provided a fitting epilogue to the life of the man who, as much as anyone, made photography the complete form of expression that it is today.

A Pioneer in Color

Portrait of the Misses Sawyer

So fertile was the talent of Edward Steichen that even in brief experiments he created noteworthy pictures. One such experiment, foredoomed by technical considerations, yielded the pioneering color photographs on these and the following pages. Only one of them has been published before, and the existence of three was not even known until they turned up among his effects after his death.

These photographs are examples of the first relatively simple form of color photography, the Autochrome process invented by the French brothers Auguste and Louis Lumière. Autochromes were glass plates coated with millions of tiny grains of starch dyed in primary colors to serve as filters in the creation of color transparencies. Steichen was in Paris in 1907 when the plates came onto the market, and he was the first recognized photographer to try them. The soft, luminous colors—reminding him of stained glass—seemed made for his romantic eye, and he spent the next three years exploring the possibilities of the process. However, the complexity of converting the transparencies into prints—which he considered essential for serious work—forced him to conclude that Autochromes were unsuitable for professional photographers. But the still lifes and gentle portraits he had done served to make a historic point. After viewing them Alfred Stieglitz declared that color photography was "an accomplished fact."

Bouquet with Cloth Background

Selma Stieglitz Schubart In the Style of Sargent

Portrait of the Portraitist Gertrude Kasebier

Lady in Fur Coat

Alfred Stieglitz with his Journal ''Camera Work''

Milestones

Dean Brown: 1936-1973

In a tragically ironic accident, Dean Brown fell to his death in July while photographing a remote waterfall at sunset in the White Mountains of New Hampshire. His brief career as a professional photographer had earned him a reputation for great expertise and resourcefulness in the depiction of wilderness landscapes. He often waited until sunset or dawn to get the effect that he desired. He once wrote, "My main effort in photographing landscape is to achieve a sense of place—not just take pretty scenics."

An experienced woodsman, Brown would sometimes hike and camp for days to locate the powerful scenes that typified his work. He was one of the few photographers who processed color film himself, making exhibition prints by his own dye-transfer process to recreate the warm reds and browns of a sunset in Arizona's Navaho Indian Reservation *(right, top)* or the cool blues of a shore scene in Glacier Bay, Alaska *(right, bottom)*. Away from the wilderness, Brown often infused his pictures with a brooding quality by choosing the soft light at the margins of the day. In the picture on the opposite page, an elegant garden pool in Arizona is darkened by late-afternoon shadows, transforming the young woman swimming underwater into a ghostly presence.

Before he became a full-time photographer, Brown studied linguistics at Cornell University and musicology at New York University. His first professional photographs were portraits of musicians and opera singers, but he soon turned to the wilderness landscapes that preoccupied him to the very moment of his fatal accident.

Red Striped Hills, 1969

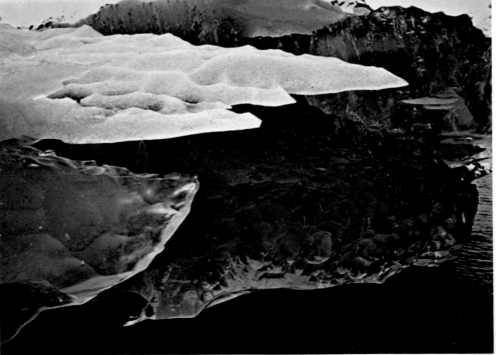

Glacial Ice, Alaska, 1971

Garden Pool, Arizona, 1973

223

Eliot Elisofon: 1911-1973

Eliot Elisofon died of a stroke in April, four months after the suspension of LIFE, the magazine he had helped shape almost from its beginning. There was more than a chronological parallel of careers, however, for Elisofon was in many respects the real-life actuality of the LIFE photographer of fiction. Quick-witted, self-assured, friend of celebrities and a celebrity in his own right, he excelled in many fields of photography: World War II battle pictures, Hollywood glamour portraits, African documentaries. When away from his camera he was a successful author, a gifted painter, a gourmet chef and an authority on primitive sculpture.

After his graduation from Fordham University in New York City in 1933, Elisofon learned the fundamentals of documentary photography as a member—and later president—of the Photo League, an organization of youthful photographers who were encouraged to seek meaningful subjects in the city streets; one of Elisofon's earliest efforts was the sensitive depiction of the sidewalk photographer at right. Elisofon joined the staff of LIFE in 1942, and over the next 23 years his assignments were to take him more than two million miles in six continents. His mastery of the evocative powers of photography ranged from clear-eyed objectivity—as in the view of an ocean-torn Atlantic beach at center—to feats of studio artifice. For a picture of actor Roddy McDowall *(far right)* in the role of the spirit Ariel from Shakespeare's *The Tempest,* he employed blue and green lights, two filters and a long exposure to obtain the unearthly effect that he felt the portrayal required.

Sidewalk Photographer, 1936

Hog Island, Virginia, 1946

Roddy McDowall as Ariel, 1957

225

Stanley Wayman: 1927-1973

It was Stan Wayman's belief that "the chief ingredients in good wildlife photography are luck and patience." He made good use of both characteristics —and his own artistry—until a fatal heart attack prematurely ended his career last March at the age of 45.

Wayman once spent more than two months in the arctic wasteland of Baffin Island in order to find and photograph a family of rare white wolves. On another assignment, he crouched from dusk to dawn in an Indian jungle to get close-ups of tigers in their natural habitat; one of his rewards was a spectacular view of a perfectly camouflaged tiger *(opposite)* pausing in the jungle grass at sunset. But if patience and luck were ingredients in his photographic successes, his own quick reflexes and keen eye counted for more. On one occasion he was photographing the denizens of a coral reef at Palau Island in the Pacific when he spotted a native dugout crossing a reef lagoon; instinctively he pressed the shutter release to capture the unusual composition of blues, greens and grays at right.

The qualities that enabled him to record memorable views of remote corners of the world served him well in a variety of assignments as a photojournalist. For many of his 15 years with LIFE, Wayman was assigned to the White House, where he photographed the activities of four Presidents. He risked his life to record violent uprisings in Panama and Algeria. And, back in Florida where he had spent boyhood days photographing birds, he stoically endured six days of brutal heat to capture the flight of a different kind of bird —an early space missile.

Palau Lagoon, 1969

Tiger at Sunset, 1965

Ugo Mulas: 1928-1973

The death of Italian photographer Ugo Mulas of cancer in March, at the age of 44, cut short the career of one of the preeminent chroniclers of the world of modern art. A police officer's son who dropped out of law school to lead a bohemian life in Milan, Mulas dabbled in both painting and poetry before turning to photography. He formed a small photo agency with two friends and a borrowed camera, but was virtually unknown outside of Milan until 1954. In that year, Mulas achieved his first important success when he photographed artists attending the Venice Biennale, one of Europe's most prestigious exhibitions of contemporary painting and sculpture. His ability to understand and communicate the highly intellectual concepts and the novel techniques of modern art soon earned him widespread acclaim.

One of his most effective stratagems was to show the artist in the process of creation. To convey the intensity with which the late Lucio Fontana gouged, punctured and sliced canvases to produce "spatial art," Mulas depicted the silhouetted artist *(opposite, left)* completing a razor slash that carries the impact of an exclamation point—which it resembles. Fascinated by the time-arresting sculptural method of George Segal, who makes plaster casts of live models, Mulas showed a male model and the empty cocoon of a woman in almost classical repose *(opposite, right)*.

Mulas was equally imaginative in examining his own artistic role. In the self-portrait at right he used his shadow and mirrored image "to see myself at the same time as I'm seeing"—not once, but twice in a single exposure.

Taking a Photo, 1971

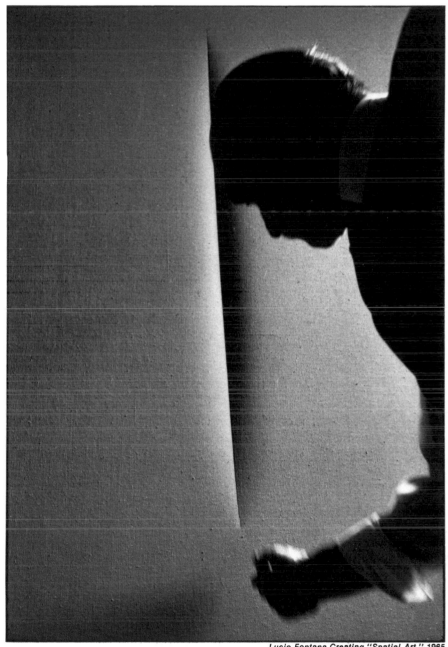

Lucio Fontana Creating "Spatial Art," 1965

Plaster Cast Images, 1964

Smithsonian's Replica of Wagon Darkroom

"Detective" Wrist Camera

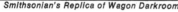

Photography Hall at Smithsonian

The Smithsonian Institution, that venerable repository of Americana, has taken photography into its purview. In September it officially opened a new Hall of Photography, an 8,000-square-foot gallery that deals with photography as an art, a science and a means of communication. Some exhibits are designed so that a visitor involves himself. He can crank old machines to watch 19th Century predecessors of the movies or fit his own camera to a strobe flash setup that enables him to get a stop-action picture freezing a small, rapidly rotating disk. He can even sit for his own tintype portrait —made by the now antiquated instant-picture process that was employed by street photographers for generations.

With the newly opened hall, the Smithsonian becomes the second largest photography museum in the world (after the International Museum of Photography at George Eastman House in Rochester, New York). Its archives, from which selections will be drawn for exhibition in a small gallery, include several hundred thousand pictures— among them the original glass negatives of Mathew Brady's portraits of political leaders of the Lincoln administration and 200,000 news pictures of the 1920s and 1930s, most of them yet-to-be-catalogued.

Perhaps even more in line with the Smithsonian's reputation as the nation's attic is its collection of antique equipment, some original, some replicas. Among the originals are the New York *Daily News* collection of disguised detective cameras *(above, right),* the camera used by Samuel F. B. Morse, the telegraph inventor, to make daguerreotypes in New York in 1839 (the year photography was first announced to the world), and an 1840 model of a mirror camera devised by the photographer Alexander S. Wolcott. Many of the replicas are in dioramas that recreate early photographic laboratories: one used about 1888 by the Eastman Dry Plate and Film Company, where the first Kodak snapshots were sent to be developed; another in the wagon driven by Roger Fenton as he covered the Crimean War *(above, left);* and another in the room where William Henry Fox Talbot developed the modern negative-positive photographic process.

A Master's Return
It was the same site and the same eye at the camera, but a different image showed up in the viewfinder. For 70 years had passed since Jacques-Henri Lartigue, then age seven, began making the pictures of turn-of-the-century life that have charmed modern viewers. In February he was back in the Bois de Boulogne *(top right),* this time photographing Parisian elegance, 1973-style, for the German magazine *Die Zeit.*

Lartigue's photographs of pre-World War I Paris, taken as a boyhood hobby, were unknown until The Museum of Modern Art and LIFE magazine brought them to public notice in 1963; then they were an instant hit for the way they captured the essence of that carefree era, when gentle ladies in feathered hats, hobble skirts and giant muffs walked diminutive dogs *(bottom right).* When *Die Zeit* asked Lartigue to photograph contemporary clothes, he set up his camera in his familiar location, confident that, while fashions have changed and pants have replaced hobble skirts, the strollers in the Bois would be as photogenic as they were before World War I.

A Photography Magazine—in Spain
A lively new photography magazine cropped up in Spain, a conservative country not heretofore remarkable for interest in photography. The magazine, called *Nueva Lente* (new lens), carries some news about photographic equipment, but focuses primarily on the work of photographers. It has a rather bi-

Lartigue's Bois de Boulogne, 1973

Lartigue's Bois de Boulogne, 1913

zarre format: headlines, text and pictures are designed in various shapes and sizes and set on the page at different angles. Articles range from the serious, such as features on important photographers who are internationally known, to the tongue-in-cheek; one recent issue carried a spoof on the question of whether or not witches really exist, and followed the text with 10 pages of photographs of women, all of them scenes of fantasy.

The Burgeoning Cooperatives
In Paris, seven French photojournalists join forces under the name Banzai and tackle an ambitious project: capturing the mood of France on Bastille Day, its most important national holiday.

In London, four young photography-school students—an Englishman, an American, an Australian and an Israeli —pool their blossoming talents in a group called Exit. As an experiment "to see if and how we can work together," they document Wapping, a grimy dockside community *(right)*. It turns out so well that they receive a grant for a documentary on the entire city of London.

In Chicago, three black freelances unite as Visual Associates in order to compete more effectively for assignments in a white-oriented marketplace.

These three groups formed in 1973, a year in which a trend toward small cooperatives gained momentum. Each one formed works differently.

Banzai began with a $180 stake from each of its seven members. All fees are turned over to the group, with half earmarked for expenses and the other half divided equally among all members.

Exit's four members each contributed $575 to form a partnership that is

Mrs. King and Mrs. Selking, Wapping Gardens

The Wilsons and the Doyles of London's Wapping

sustained by weekly contributions from earnings. The three members of Visual Associates contribute 10 per cent of their earnings to pay for a telephone answering service, mail drop and promotional catalog. Members still handle individual and group assignments.

But what may work in Paris, London and Chicago does not necessarily work elsewhere. In Rome a promising venture called Reprom failed after only three months because its four members could not agree on assignments and

work-sharing. A San Francisco group called Jeroboam also began to splinter shortly after its creation. In a profession that prizes individualism, the casualty rate for cooperatives runs high. But groups will continue to form as photographers merge their skills and incomes in order to survive—and, with luck, to prosper.

New Look for Photokina
Every second year, crowds of visitors —more than a quarter of a million in

Mr. Berry and Trixie, Prusom Street, Wapping

1972—flock to Cologne, Germany, to see Photokina, the world's largest photographic fair, where some 700 manufacturers and dealers in photographic equipment market their wares and hundreds of photographers show their pictures. The visitors will find something different when they turn up next time, for the fair will be remodeled for 1974. It will be divided into two halves: the technology section will be located, as usual, on the fairgrounds just across the Rhine River from the center of the city, but the photographic gallery will be moved from the fairgrounds to Cologne's art museum, the *Kunsthalle*.

The changes are intended to reduce crowding and make it easier for visitors to follow up their special interests. Tourists attracted by photographic art will find the downtown location of the gallery more convenient—and presumably will be kept out of the way of the fairgrounds businessmen, whose primary aim is to buy and sell equipment, not look at picture exhibitions.

Photo Fair behind the Iron Curtain

Behind the Iron Curtain in Prague a photographic fair called Interkamera, smaller than West Germany's Photokina *(above)*, held its fourth biennial exhibition in April. Of the 65 firms participating, some were from Czechoslovakia, East Germany and Poland, but West Germany and Japan dominated the exhibition halls.

Most of the displays featured professional equipment, since professional photography is financed by the state, and few ordinary citizens have enough spending money for such fripperies as amateur photography. But the Czech public visited the fair all the same, and there they clustered around two of the exhibits: one showed color television —Czechoslovakia still has only black and white. The other featured Polaroid's SX-70 camera; self-developing color photographs are still a novelty in Soviet-bloc countries.

Camera Collecting—A Growing Fad

When the members of several regional camera clubs met in Columbus, Ohio, in May to form the Photographic Historical Society of America, the gathering underscored the new interest in antique-camera collecting. At least 16 different cities and towns across the country have collectors' clubs; in 1968 only the one in Columbus existed. Most of the clubs issue newsletters, and other newsletters—some with circulations in the thousands—are issued independently; in addition photography magazines have begun to carry columns on camera collecting, as well as ads offering cameras for sale or swap.

The rapid growth of the hobby has had a predictable effect on the value of most old cameras. The Univex A, a tiny plastic-backed camera that cost 39 cents when it was marketed during the 1930s, was worth four dollars in 1973. A camera called the Compass, manufactured by the Le Coultre Watchmaking Company in Switzerland, sold for $150 when it was new in 1938. In the early 1960s the same camera cost about $250. Today, if one can be found, the vintage camera goes for $1,000.

But the prices for real antiques are even more staggering. One man bought a daguerreotype camera at a Salvation Army sale in 1968 for five dollars; in 1973 it was valued at $5,000.

The collectors look for cameras that are rare or that represent a milestone in technological development. In short, that means anything from the daguerreotype period (about 1840); anything from the wet-plate period (1851-1867); anything made prior to World War I (after which came the 35mm camera and with it a new era for photography); almost anything that spawned a successful line (an example of the original 35mm camera, the Leica A, could bring $400 in 1973); and the first model of practically any camera, whether its line has survived or not.

Photography Courses in High School
The ever-increasing interest in photography began to reach into high-school study programs as *Scholastic Magazines,* publishers of classroom materi-

Henri Cartier-Bresson's ''Greek Girl'' for High-School Study

als for half a century, offered photography appreciation courses designed for grades 10 through 12. The courses, titled *Images of Man,* are really combination packages of recordings and filmstrips or slides. They present the work of eight practicing photographers —Cornell Capa, Bruce Davidson, Donald McCullin, W. Eugene Smith, William Albert Allard, Henri Cartier-Bresson *(above),* Brian Lanker and Eliot Porter —who describe their approaches in the recorded narration. The courses, which were developed by Sheila Turner Seed together with Cornell Capa, represent a cross section of photographic styles and viewpoints.

The Hill-Adamson Affair
The value now placed on old photographs was proved by an uproar when London's Royal Academy of Art attempted to auction photographs by two Scottish pioneers, David Octavius Hill, a painter, and Robert Adamson, an engineer, who collaborated as photographers between 1843 and 1848. Public outcry halted the sale.

The collection is unique because Hill and Adamson created sensitive portraits that were among the earliest photographs ever made of ordinary people engaged in everyday tasks—in this case fishing folk. When Adamson died at the age of 27, Hill abandoned photography, returned to painting and donated to the Royal Academy albums containing 258 prints that he and his partner had made together.

There the photographs were stored, forgotten, for 125 years. Even after they were rediscovered, they attracted little notice—until the Academy sought to raise some money by auctioning them off. That was bad news to British connoisseurs of photography who

cruise from New York to West Africa and back aboard the S.S. *Canberra;* its deck became so crowded with photographic and astronomical gear that the travelers called it the Tripod National Forest *(left).* That one ship carried over 1,800 passengers, some 40 of whom lectured the others on what they might expect to see and on how to get the best pictures during the few minutes when the moon obscured the sun.

The equipment used on the eclipse cruise included a wide variety of telescopes, lenses and cameras. Most pictures were taken with 35mm SLRs loaded with ordinary high-speed color-slide film but fitted with long lenses to produce large images of the sun. Even the relatively short lenses were of 300mm focal length and some giants of 2,000mm were used. The most special requirement was a heavy neutral-density filter—to prevent overexposure (and infrared-ray damage to the shutter) when the camera lens was pointed directly at the unobscured sun—and considerable manual dexterity. Exposure had to be adjusted repeatedly during the few minutes of rapid light change as the moon passed over the sun; for the dimmest moments at totality, the filter had to be taken off, then replaced as the sun reappeared and the light brightened.

But the biggest problem in photographing the eclipse, commented one expert, was the spectacular nature of the event. Toward the climax, the sight of the blackened sun surrounded by its fiery corona so stunned some of the photographers that they stood hushed beside their cameras and momentarily forgot the point of their journey, to take pictures of the eclipse.

feared that the prints would go to American or Japanese buyers, who in recent years have been acquiring antiques and art all over the world. In a surge of indignation, angry Britishers deluged the Academy and the newspapers with letters demanding that the sale be called off on the grounds that the photographs ought to be preserved as a national treasure.

At length the Academy yielded to public opinion and canceled the auction—not without having to pay Sotheby's, the dealer engaged to handle the sale, $7,000 in forfeited commissions. Academy officials then began a search for a "suitable"—which meant British —buyer. The Academy was lucky—and so was the British public. In January an anonymous benefactor came forth with $75,000, and bought the pictures for the National Portrait Gallery where they were exhibited.

Camera Cruise to an Eclipse

One of the heavens' rarest phenomena, a solar eclipse lasting more than seven minutes, occurred on June 30, and perhaps no eclipse in history has been so thoroughly documented on film. To witness the event from various locations in coastal and inland Africa, where the viewing was best, thousands of people traveled to the Dark Continent from at least 28 countries—most notably the United States, Britain, France, Russia, Japan and West Germany. Among them were amateur and professional astronomers, solar physicists, space officials, marine biologists, teachers, students and assorted tourists. And practically all of them carried cameras, to record not only the eclipse but also the scenery and people they saw at the various African observation sites.

Perhaps the most ambitious of all these expeditions was a two-week-long

Calendar

Photographic exhibitions, meetings and other events of 1974 are listed below according to the city and the month in which they were scheduled to take place. Exact dates within each month should be ascertained from sponsors of events.

JANUARY
CHICAGO, The Art Institute. Exhibition: Richard Nickel.
NEW YORK CITY, The Jewish Museum. Exhibition: Bedrich Grunzweig (through March).
OAKLAND, CALIFORNIA, Oakland Museum. Exhibition: "Mirror of California," daguerreotypes from 1847 to 1867.
OMAHA, NEBRASKA, Joslyn Art Museum. Exhibition: Thomas Langdon, Margaret Moore and Raymond Phillips.
PALO ALTO, CALIFORNIA, The F/Stop Gallery. Exhibition: Ken Light.
SAN FRANCISCO, San Francisco Museum of Art. Exhibitions: Ronald C. Stark and Phil Trager (through February).
*****WASHINGTON, D.C., The Corcoran Gallery of Art.** Exhibition: "Man Ray Photo Graphics," from the collection of A. H. Crane *(pages 71-81).*
Lunn Gallery. Exhibitions: Bill Brandt and Ansel Adams.
Smithsonian Institution. Exhibition: "American Masters of Photography" (through May).

FEBRUARY
NEW YORK CITY, Cooper Union. Lecture Series: "Photography for Advertising" (for advanced amateurs).
OAKLAND, CALIFORNIA, Oakland Museum. Exhibition: Van Deren Coke (through March).
PROVIDENCE, RHODE ISLAND, Rhode Island School of Design. Exhibition: Thomas T. Ebbers.
TORONTO, ONTARIO, Baldwin Street Gallery. Exhibition: Paul Rayner.

MARCH
BOSTON, Boston Museum of Fine Arts. Exhibitions: "20th Century Photographs from the Museum's Collection"; "Pictorialist Photographs of the Early 20th Century"; "Photography-Printmaking" (all through April); "Private Realities," recent American photography (through May).
CARBONDALE, ILLINOIS, Southern Illinois University. Exhibition: "Synthetic Color."
FLORENCE, ITALY, Palazzo Vecchio. Exhibition: Nunes Vais.
HOUSTON, TEXAS, Museum of Fine Arts. Exhibition: Geoff Winningham (through April).
LONDON, The Royal Photographic Society. Symposium: Early Photographic Processes and the Conservation of Early Photos.
LOUISVILLE, KENTUCKY, Center for Photographic Studies. Exhibition: Joseph Jachna *(pages 110-117).*
NEW YORK CITY, Floating Foundation of Photography. Exhibition: "Women Photographers," a group show.
The Museum of Modern Art. Exhibition: "New Japanese Photography," (through May).
Sonnabend Gallery. Exhibition: Horst.
NORTH VANCOUVER, BRITISH COLUMBIA, The Gallery of Photography. Exhibition: Atget.
ROCHESTER, NEW YORK, Rochester Institute of Technology. Conference: Society for Photographic Education.

APRIL
CHICAGO, The Art Institute. Exhibition: Manuel Alvarez Bravo.
*****FLINT, MICHIGAN, Flint Institute of Art.** Exhibition: Yousuf Karsh (through May).
HAMBURG, GERMANY, Museum für Kunst und Gewerbe. Exhibition: Fritz Kempe. **Staatliche Landesbildstelle.** Exhibition: Willy Hengl.
LONDON, National Portrait Gallery. Exhibition: Sir Benjamin Stone (through May).
OAKLAND, CALIFORNIA, Oakland Museum. Exhibition: Imogen Cunningham.
NEW YORK CITY, The Metropolitan Museum of Art. Exhibition: Ansel Adams (through June).
The Witkin Gallery. Exhibitions: Judy Dater and Jack Welpott.
PARMA, ITALY, Palazzo della Pilotta. Exhibition: Luigi Veronesi.

MAY
ALBUQUERQUE, NEW MEXICO, University of New Mexico. Exhibition: "291," a re-creation of Alfred Stieglitz' New York gallery.
Quivira Book Shop and Photograph Gallery. Exhibition: Photogravures of Alaska and Eskimos, by Robert Flaherty.
BOSTON, The Carl Siembab Gallery of Photography. Exhibition: Nick Stephens.
DETROIT, MICHIGAN, The Detroit Institute of Arts. Exhibition: Diane Arbus (through June).
ELLENSBURG, WASHINGTON, Central Washington State College. Exhibition: "New Photographics/74."
NEW YORK CITY, The Jewish Museum. Exhibition: "Jerusalem, City of Mankind" (through October).
Light Gallery. Exhibitions: Aaron Siskind and John Gutmann (through May).
PARIS, Galerie de la Société Française de Photographie. Exhibition: "The French Cup," amateur competition.
WASHINGTON, D.C., Library of Congress. Exhibition: "Color in the Graphic Arts" (through October).

JUNE
COMO, ITALY, Villa Olmo. Exhibition: "Colors in Transparency," an international competition.
NEW YORK CITY, Robert Schoelkopf Gallery. Exhibition: "The Portrait in the History of Photography."
ROCHESTER, NEW YORK, Light Impressions Gallery. Exhibition: Arnold Gassan.
SAN FRANCISCO, Focus Gallery. Exhibition: John Dunlap.
WASHINGTON, D.C., Smithsonian Institution. Exhibition: Washington Photographers (through September).

JULY
ARLES, FRANCE, Festival d'Arles. Exhibitions: Ansel Adams and George A. Tice. Conference: "The Liberties of Photography."
CHALON-SUR-SAÔNE, FRANCE, Europhot. Exhibition: "Photography in the World of Visual Communication" (through September).
GRINNELL, IOWA, East Street Gallery. Exhibition: Larry Frank.
LONDON, National Portrait Gallery. Exhibition: "Dr. Barnardo's Children."
The Photographers' Gallery. Exhibition: Cecil Beaton.
ROCHESTER, NEW YORK, George Eastman House. Exhibition: "Power to Persuade" (through September).

AUGUST
HAMBURG, Staatliche Landesbildstelle. Exhibition: Peter Thomann.
SIEGEN, GERMANY, Galerie Der Stadt. Exhibition: Ralph Gibson (through September).

SEPTEMBER
COLOGNE, Photokina. Exhibition and Trade Fair.
Fotogalerie Wilde. Exhibition: Josef Sudek (through October).
LONDON, Kodak Gallery. Exhibition: "Romantic Landscapes."
NEW YORK CITY, Niekrug Gallery. Exhibitions: Brian Lanker *(page 184)* and "Dust Bowl."
PASADENA, CALIFORNIA, The Pasadena Art Museum. Exhibition: "Photography Since 1950."

OCTOBER
OAKLAND, CALIFORNIA, Oakland Museum. Exhibition: "California Landscapes" (through November).
PARIS, The Museum of Modern Art. Exhibition: French Group of Free Expression.
TURIN, ITALY, Società Fotografica Sub-Alpina. Exhibition: "Photocolor Festival," color competition winners.
WASHINGTON, D.C., Smithsonian Institution. Exhibition: "Multiple Images" (through December).

NOVEMBER
NEW YORK CITY, Whitney Museum of American Art. Exhibition: "American Photography" (through January).
ROCHESTER, NEW YORK, George Eastman House. Exhibition: "Invitational Exhibition" (through December).

DECEMBER
HAMBURG, Staatliche Landesbildstelle. Exhibition: Robert Lebeck.
LONDON, Hayward Gallery. Exhibition: "Anthology of British Photographers 1839-1974."

* Traveling Exhibition

Bibliography

General
Editors of TIME-LIFE BOOKS, *Life Library of Photography*. TIME-LIFE BOOKS, 1970-1972.
Focal Press, *The Focal Encyclopedia of Photography*. Focal Press, Ltd., 1965.
Gernsheim, Helmut, *Creative Photography: Aesthetic Trends 1839-1960*. Faber & Faber Ltd., 1962.
History of Photography. Oxford University Press, 1955.
The History of Photography from the Camera Obscura to the Beginning of the Modern Era. McGraw-Hill, 1969.
Newhall, Beaumont, *The History of Photography: from 1839 to the Present Day*. The Museum of Modern Art, 1964.
—and Nancy, *Masters of Photography*. Harry N. Abrams, 1969.

Special Essays
Bull, Clarence Sinclair, *Faces of Hollywood*. A. S. Barnes and Company, 1968.
Carroll, John S., *Color Film and Processing Data Book*. American Photographic Book Publishing Co., Inc., 1972.
Census of Business, Selected Services, Miscellaneous Subjects. 1967 ed. U.S. Department of Commerce, Bureau of the Census, 1971.
Coke, Van Deren, *The Painter and the Photograph*. University of New Mexico Press, 1972.
Elisofon, Eliot:
Color Photography. The Viking Press, Inc., 1961.
The Hill/Adamson Albums. Times Newspapers Limited, 1973.
Horrell, Dr. C. William, *A Survey of Motion Picture, Still Photography, and Graphic Arts Instruction*, 4th ed. Eastman Kodak Company, 1971.
A Survey of Photographic Instruction, 3rd ed. Eastman Kodak Company, 1968.
Lartigue, Jacques-Henri:
Boyhood Photos of J.-H. Lartigue. Ami Guichard, 1966.
Levin, Phyllis Lee, *The Wheels of Fashion*. Doubleday and Company, Inc., 1965.
Mannheim, L. Andrew & Viscount Hanworth, *D. A. Spencer's Colour Photography in Practice*, rev. ed. Focal Press, Ltd., 1969.
Mit Kamera, Pinsel und Spritzpistore, Städtische Kunsthalle Recklinghausen, 1973.
Mulas, Ugo:
La Fotografia. Giulio Einaudi, editore s.p.a., Turin, Italy, 1973.
—and Pietro Consagra, *Fotografare l'Arte*. Fratelli Fabbri Editori, Milan, Italy, 1973.
—and Alan Solomon, *New York: The New Art Scene*. Holt, Rinehart and Winston, 1967.
About Mulas:
Ugo Mulas, Immagine e Testi. Università di Parma, Parma, Italy, 1973.
Ray, Man:
Self Portrait. Little, Brown and Company, 1963.
About Ray:
Man Ray. Los Angeles County Museum of Art, Lytton Gallery, 1966.
Man Ray. The Metropolitan Museum of Art, 1973.
Scharf, Aaron, *Art and Photography*. The Penguin Press, London, England, 1968.
Steichen, Edward:
A Life in Photography. Doubleday and Company, Inc., 1963.
About Steichen:
Sandburg, Carl, *Steichen the Photographer*. Harcourt Brace, 1929.
Steichen the Photographer. The Museum of Modern Art, Doubleday and Company, Inc., 1961.
Szarkowski, John, ed., *From the Picture Press*. The Museum of Modern Art, 1973.

Periodicals
Aperture. Aperture, Inc., Millerton, New York.
The British Journal of Photography. Henry Greenwood & Co., London, England.
Camera. C. J. Bucher Ltd., Lucerne, Switzerland.
Camera 35. American Express Publishing Corp., New York City.
Camera Work (1903-1917), Alfred Stieglitz, New York City.
Creative Camera. Coo Press Ltd., London, England.
Esquire. Esquire Inc., New York City.
Exposure. Journal of the Society for Photographic Education, New York City.
Harper's Bazaar. The Hearst Corporation, New York City.
Infinity (1952-1973), American Society of Magazine Photographers, New York City.
Modern Photography. Billboard Publications, Inc., New York City.
National Geographic Magazine. National Geographic Society, Washington, D.C.
PHOTO WORLD. Photo Journal, Inc., New York City.
The Photographic Journal. The Royal Photographic Society, London, England.
Photographic Magazine. Petersen Publishing Co., Los Angeles, California.
Popular Photography. Ziff-Davis Publishing Co., New York City.
Vogue. The Condé Nast Publications Inc., New York City.
Zoom. Publicness, Paris, France.

Acknowledgments

For their help, the editors are indebted to Peter C. Bunnell, Princeton University, N.J., and to Walter Clark, Rochester, N.Y.
The editors also thank: In the Americas—Adriane Berner, New York City; Donald P. Blake, *Graphic Antiquarian*, Wilmington, N.C.; Carol Brown, New York City; Harry Callahan, Rhode Island School of Design, Providence; Steve Camp, Beseler Photo Marketing, Florham Park, N.J.; Bobbi Carrey, Cambridge, Mass.; Ben and Howard Chapnick, Black Star Publishing Company, New York City; Carl Chiarenza, Boston Univ.; Philip L. Condax, Rochester, N.Y.; Arnold H. Crane, Chicago; Fred A. Demarest, School of Public Communications, Syracuse Univ., N.Y.; Orlan Donaldson, Bethlehem Steel Corp., Bethlehem, Pa.; Alfred Eisenstaedt, New York City; Susanne Goldstein, Rapho Guillumette, New York City; Rodger L. Grimes, Eastman Kodak Company, Rochester, N.Y.; Norman Griner, Horn-Griner Inc., New York City; W. Scott Grover, Eastman Kodak Company, Rochester, N.Y.; David Haberstich, Smithsonian Institution, Washington, D.C.; Edward Handler, Art Center College of Design, Los Angeles; Robert Heinecken, Univ. of California, Los Angeles; Hiro, New York City; Ryzsard Horowitz, New York City; Dr. C. William Horrell, Southern Illinois Univ., Carbondale; Yale Joel, Croton-on-Hudson, N.Y.; William F. Kuykendall, School of Journalism, Univ. of Missouri, Columbia; Richard Lawton, Providence, R.I.; Jerome Liebling, Hampshire College, Amherst, Mass.; Dennis Longwell, The Museum of Modern Art, New York City; Eaton S. Lothrop Jr., New York City; Dan McCoy, Lime Rock, Conn.; Angus McDougall, School of Journalism, Univ. of Missouri, Columbia; Phil Marco, New York City; Grace Mayer, The Museum of Modern Art, New York City; Gjon Mili, New York City; Weston Naef, The Metropolitan Museum of Art, New York City; Beaumont Newhall, Univ. of New Mexico, Albuquerque; Dorothy Norman, New York City; Frederick Quellmalz, Professional Photographers of America, Inc., Des Plaines, Ill.; Roger D. Reed, Eastman Kodak Company, Rochester, N.Y.; Arthur Rothstein, *Parade*, New York City; Skip Rozin, New York City; James M. Sahlstrand, Central Washington State College, Ellensburg, Wash.; Jason Schneider, *Modern Photography*, New York City; Martin L. Scott, Eastman Kodak Company, Rochester, N.Y.; Sheila Turner Seed, *Scholastic Magazines*, New York City; William S. Shoemaker, Rochester Institute of Technology, N.Y.; Aaron Siskind, Rhode Island School of Design, Providence; Harris G. Smith, School of Public Communication, Boston Univ.; Joanna Taub Steichen, New York City; Richard A. Steinberg, New York City; John Szarkowski, The Museum of Modern Art, New York City; Ron Tunison, Guidance Associates, Pleasantville, N.Y.; Jerry N. Uelsmann, Univ. of Florida, Gainesville; Wolf von dem Bussche, New York City; Bob Walsh, New York City; Minor White, Massachusetts Institute of Technology, Cambridge.
In Asia—W. Eugene Smith, Tokyo; Yoshio Watanabe, Japan Photographers Assoc., Tokyo.
In Europe—Pierre Bel, Galérie Nikon, Paris;

Gail Buckland, The Royal Photographic Society of Great Britain, London; Augusto Baracchini Caputi, Livorno; Marie-Loup Sanchez Cascado, Paris; Lanfranco Colombo, *Il Diaframma-Fotografia Italiana,* Milan; Roger Doloy, Club Photographique de Paris-Les 30x40, Paris; Oreste Ferrari, Gabinetto Fotografico Nazionale, Rome; L. Fritz Gruber, Photokina, Cologne; Dr. Jean-Claude Lamielle, CNRI, Paris; Jean-Claude Lemagny, Cabinet des Estampes, Bibliothèque Nationale, Paris; Richard Kalvar, Agence Viva, Paris; Guy Knoché, Association des Gens d'Image, Paris; Guy Marineau, Agence Banzai, Paris; Michel Quetin, Archives Nationales, Paris; Arturo Quintavalle, Università Degli Studi, Parma; Christiane Raimond-Dityvon, Agence Viva, Paris; Man Ray, Paris; Professor Otto Steinert, Universität und Gesammthochschule, Essen.

Picture Credits *Credits from left to right are separated by semicolons, from top to bottom by dashes.*

COVER—Joseph Jachna; David Hamilton, reproduced by permission of William Morrow & Company, Inc. from *Sisters* by David Hamilton & Alain Robbe-Grillet, copyright © 1972 by Swan Productions, Switzerland.

The Documentary: 11 through 19—Neal Slavin. 20 through 27—© Pete Turner. 29 through 36 —Garry Winogrand.

The Year's Books: Pages 39 through 45 courtesy Richard Lawton. 39—Clarence S. Bull. 41—No credit. 42—George Hurrell. 43—Eugene Robert Richee. 44—No credit. 45—Ernest A. Bachrach. 46—Rennie George. 47—Clarence E. Eastmond. 48—Theron Taylor. 49—Anthony Barboza. 51,52, 53—Bill Owens. 54 through 57—Gilbert Wight Tilton and Fred W. Record, courtesy © Mark Silber, Dimension, Inc. 58 through 61—David Hamilton, reproduced by permission of William Morrow & Company, Inc. from *Sisters* by David Hamilton & Alain Robbe-Grillet, copyright © 1972 by Swan Productions, Switzerland. Pages 63 through 67 except page 65 courtesy The Museum of Modern Art, New York. 63—Peter Henry Emerson. 64—E. J. Bellocq. 65—Manuel Alvarez Bravo. 66—Barbara Morgan. 67 —William Klein.

The Major Shows: 71 through 81—Man Ray, ADAGP 1973 by French Reproduction Rights Inc., courtesy Arnold Crane, copied by Paulus Leeser. 82—George Breitner, courtesy Rijksbureau voor Kunsthistorische Documentatie, The Hague. 83—Courtesy Stedelijk Museum, Amsterdam. 85—William Henry Fox Talbot, courtesy Collection Otto Steinert; Hippolyte Bayard, courtesy Collection Otto Steinert—Thomas Eakins, courtesy Philadelphia Museum of Art, Gift of Charles Bregler. 86—László Moholy-Nagy, courtesy Collection Otto Steinert. 87—Herbert Bayer, courtesy Collection Otto Steinert. 88—Left, Foto H. E. Kiessling; Right, Foto Mahrholz, courtesy D. K. Brose, Munich. 89,90—Courtesy O. K. Harris Gallery, New York. 91—Foto Fred Wirz, courtesy Provoslav Sovák. 92—Courtesy Bykert Gallery. 93—Foto Santvoort. 95—Arthur Fellig ("Weegee") from Photoworld, courtesy The Museum of Modern Art, New York. 96—Richard Corkery, *New York Daily News,* courtesy The Museum of Modern Art, New York. 97—Charles Hoff, *New York Daily News.* 98—Sy Seidman Photos, courtesy The Museum of Modern Art, New York. 99—Ed Morgan, *Pittsburgh Sun-Telegraph,* courtesy The Museum of Modern Art, New York. 100—Ted Needham, United Press International, courtesy The Museum of Modern Art, New York—*New York Daily News,* courtesy The Museum of Modern Art, New York. 101 —Dick Peare from Photoworld, courtesy The Museum of Modern Art, New York. 102—Len Detrick, *New York Daily News,* courtesy The Museum of Modern Art, New York. 103—*New York Daily News,* courtesy The Museum of Modern Art, New York. 104—Photographs on this page have appeared previously on pages 95 through 103.

Discoveries: Leo Rubenfine; Claudine Guéniot —Enrico Natali; Terry Wild. 109—Courtesy Jean-Claude Lemagny; Courtesy Shoji Yamagishi; Alex Jamison—Arne Folkedal; Yan; Courtesy Daniela Mrázková. 110—Enrico Natali. 111 through 117—Joseph Jachna. 118 through 125 —Claudine Guéniot. 126 through 133—Terry Wild. 134—Leo Rubenfine. 135 through 139 —Marcia Resnick. 140—Marcia Resnick, courtesy Lee Witkin.

The Marketplace: 143—Ryszard Horowitz, photographed for AC&R Advertising, Inc. for Reed & Barton. 144—Ted Wathen. 145—Luther Smith Jr.—Arno Rafael Minkkinen. 146—© Arnold Newman. 148,149—Hiro, courtesy *Harper's Bazaar* © Hearst Corporation 1973. 150,151—Wolf von dem Bussche, courtesy Esterline Corporation. 153—Harvey Lloyd. 154,155—Jay Maisel, courtesy Schlumberger Limited. 156—Aaron Siskind—Harry Callahan. 157—Jerry N. Uelsmann. 158 through 166—Luis Villota.

The Annual Awards: 169,170,171—William Bornefeld. 172—Left, Martin Benjamin; right, James Barker. 173—Simon Cherpitel. 174—Cliff Feulner. 175—Richard Albertine. 176—Clara Bulkley. 177—Gregory Pile. 179—Albert Visage from Jacana. 180—Co Rentmeester, TIME-LIFE Picture Agency, © 1972 Time Incorporated. 181 —John Launois from Black Star © National Geographic Society; Kurt E. Smith. 182—Bunyo Ishikawa, from *North Vietnam,* published by Asahi Shimbun Ltd., Tokyo 1973. 183—Hajime Sawatari, from *Nadia,* published by Camera Mainichi, Tokyo 1973—Koji Morooka, from *Remembrance of Tokyo,* published by Kodansha Co. Ltd., Tokyo 1972. 184—Brian Lanker, courtesy *The Topeka Capital-Journal.* 185 —Huynh Cong Ut from Wide World Photos. 186 —Clive Limpkin, *The Sun,* London, from *The Battle of Bogside,* published by Penguin Books Ltd., London 1972.

The New Technology: 189—Eva Rubinstein. 192,193—Ken Kay, drawings by Nicholas Fasciano. 194—Ken Kay. 195—Ken Kay except bottom right Eva Rubinstein. 196 through 199 —Fred Pleasure. 201—Minolta Corporation; Kowa American Corp. 202—Koniphoto Corporation; Yashica Inc. 203—Sinar AG, courtesy EPOI; Berkey Photo/Keystone, courtesy The Rowland Company, Inc. 205— Nikon, Inc.; Carl Zeiss. 206—Rollei, West Germany—Canon U.S.A., Inc. 207—AIC Photo, Inc.—Ernst Leitz GmbH, West Germany. 208 —Fuji Photo Film Co., Ltd., Tokyo; Camoptics Limited, Hong Kong.

Roundup: 211—Haefer Studio, Hancock, Michigan—No credit; No credit; No credit; Edward Steichen; No credit—Edward Steichen; Irving Penn, copyright © 1959 by the Condé Nast Publications Inc.; © Karsh, Ottawa, all photographs courtesy collection of Joanna Taub Steichen. 212—Edward Steichen, courtesy The Art Institute of Chicago. 213—Edward Steichen. 214—Edward Steichen, copyright © 1935, 1963 by the Condé Nast Publications Inc., courtesy collection of Joanna Taub Steichen. 215 —Edward Steichen, photographed for J. Walter Thompson Company for The Andrew Jergens Company, courtesy collection of Joanna Taub Steichen. 216—Edward Steichen, copied by Lee Boltin, courtesy The Museum of Modern Art, New York, Gift of Miss Eleanor Conway Sawyer. 217,218—Edward Steichen, courtesy collection of Joanna Taub Steichen. 219—Edward Steichen, courtesy The Metropolitan Museum of Art, Gift of Miss Georgia O'Keeffe, 1955. 220 —Edward Steichen, courtesy collection of Joanna Taub Steichen. 221—Edward Steichen, courtesy The Metropolitan Museum of Art, Gift of Miss Georgia O'Keeffe, 1955. 222,223—Dean Brown, courtesy Carol Brown. 224,225—Eliot Elisofon, TIME-LIFE Picture Agency, © 1972 Time Incorporated except far left Eliot Elisofon, courtesy Eliot Elisofon Estate. 226,227—Stan Wayman, TIME-LIFE Picture Agency, © 1972 Time Incorporated. 228,229—Ugo Mulas, courtesy Antonia Mulas. 230—History of Photography Collection, Smithsonian Institution. 231—Copyright © Henry Pessar, Paris —Jacques-Henri Lartigue from Rapho Guillumette. 232,233—Copyright © EXIT 1973. 234—© Henri Cartier-Bresson from Magnum. 235—Martin L. Scott.

Index *Numerals in italics indicate a photograph, painting or drawing of the subject mentioned.*

Printed in U.S.A.